MULTIETHNIC CHILDREN'S LITERATURE

D0881667

MULTIETHNIC CHILDREN'S LITERATURE

Gonzalo Ramírez, Jr., Ed.D

Jan L. Ramírez, M.Ed.

Delmar
Publishers Inc. ™

I(T)P™

NOTICE TO THE READER

Publisher does not warrant or guarantee any of the products described herein or perform any independent analysis in connection with any of the product information contained herein. Publisher does not assume, and expressly disclaims, any obligation to obtain and include information other than that provided to it by the manufacturer.

The reader is expressly warned to consider and adopt all safety precautions that might be indicated by the activities described herein and to avoid all potential hazards. By following the instructions contained herein, the reader willingly assumes all risks in connection with such instructions.

The publisher makes no representations or warranties of any kind, including but not limited to, the warranties of fitness for particular purpose or merchantability, nor are any such representations implied with respect to the material set forth herein, and the publisher takes no responsibility with respect to such material. The publisher shall not be liable for any special, consequential or exemplary damages resulting, in whole or in part, from the readers' use of, or reliance upon, this material.

Cover illustration by Alexander Hieronymus Piejko
Cover design by Bob Clarke

DELMAR STAFF

Acquisitions Editor: Erin O'Connor
Project Editor: Theresa M. Bobear
Production Coordinator: Sandra Woods
Art/Design Coordinator: Karen Kunz Kemp

For information, address Delmar Publishers Inc.
3 Columbia Circle, Box 15015
Albany, New York 12212-5015

Copyright (C) 1994 by Delmar Publishers Inc.
The trademark ITP is used under license.

All rights reserved. No part of this work may be reproduced or used in any form or by any means—graphic, electronic, or mechanical, including photocopying, recording, taping, or information storage and retrieval systems—without written permission of the publisher.

Printed in the United States of America.
Published simultaneously in Canada by Nelson Canada,
a division of the Thomson Corporation

1 2 3 4 5 6 7 8 9 10 xxx 00 99 98 97 96 95 94

Library of Congress Cataloging-in-Publication Data

Ramirez, Gonzalo.
    Multiethnic children's literature / Gonzalo Ramirez, Jr., Jan L. Ramirez. — 1st ed.
        p. cm.
    Includes index.
    ISBN 0-8273-5433-9
        1. Minorities—United States—Juvenile literature—Bibliography. 2. Hispanic Americans—Juvenile literature—Bibliography. 3. Afro-Americans—Juvenile literature—Bibliography. 4. Asian Americans—Juvenile literature—Bibliography. 5. Indians of North America—Juvenile literature—Bibliography. I. Ramirez, Jan L. II. Title.
Z1361.E4R36   1994
[E184.A1]
016.3058'00973—dc20   93-39662
                                                          CIP

Contents

Preface

Play school, Play school
What do I see?
I see the carpet
Different like me.
          María Elena Ramírez, 6 years old

This book is intended for teachers, librarians, caretakers, and all other adults who are interested in helping children gain a better understanding of our culturally different populations. James A. Banks (1992) has pointed out that multiethnic education is erroneously considered to constitute courses designed exclusively for African Americans. He contends, on the contrary, that multiethnic education encompasses the struggles, hopes, and desires of all Americans, and that multiethnic education is therefore for all Americans. Similarly, we believe that multiethnic children's literature is not only for African American, Latino, Asian American, and Native American children, but for all children. It is our hope that multiethnic children's literature will help prepare our children to function in an increasingly pluralistic society.

For the purpose of this book, the terms African American, Asian American, Latino, and Native American are used to refer to America's people of color—people from these four groups who were born in the United States or who immigrated to this country. In the annotated bibliography, the cultural group depicted in a particular book will be indicated in parentheses. If no particular group is indicated, it may be assumed that the book concerns the cultural group referred to in the chapter or section title.

A grade level for each book is also suggested. Grade levels are divided into the following groups: Grades K–2, Grades 3–5, and Grades 6–8. However, some of the books labeled Grades 3–5 are appropriate for reading aloud to kindergarten children, and some labeled Grades K–2 would be appropriate for fourth-grade students reading below grade level.

One of the major goals of *Multiethnic Children's Literature* is to serve as a resource for teachers, librarians, caretakers, and others who wish to bring quality multiethnic literature to our children. Children's literature has been enriched by books for or about African Americans, Latinos, Asian Americans, and Native Americans. Authors such as Gary Soto, Laurence Yep, John Steptoe, and Byrd Baylor have written stories that reflect the experiences of our children of color.

The titles listed in this book are not all of the books published with multiethnic themes or characters. Additional books are therefore recommended and discussed as part of the annotation of some books. Also, we have focused on current multiethnic titles. Therefore, very few pre-1980 titles are listed. The books listed are those we deem exceptional in depicting accurately the culture of America's people of color and/or in providing good role models for our children and young adults. We hope that this collection of titles will instill in our children a sense of the value of our diversity and help us all to get along.

Multiethnic Children's Literature is divided into eight chapters. The following paragraphs describe each chapter.

CHAPTER 1. WHY MULTIETHNIC CHILDREN'S LITERATURE? AN OVERVIEW

The first chapter includes a definition of multiethnic children's literature and a description of America's diversity and ethnic diversity. A brief history of multiethnic children's literature from the 1940s to the present is also provided. Professional resources that can help adults locate multiethnic children's literature are listed at the end of the chapter.

CHAPTER 2. GUIDELINES FOR SELECTING MULTIETHNIC LITERATURE

Guidelines for selecting appropriate multiethnic children's literature are outlined in this chapter. Evaluating the literary elements of a multiethnic book and the use of a second language are also discussed.

CHAPTER 3. BOOKS FOR AND ABOUT MEXICAN AMERICANS, PUERTO RICANS, AND OTHER LATINOS

This chapter begins with a discussion of the terms *Latino* and *Hispanic*. An annotated bibliography of books for or about Mexican Americans is provided. An annotated bibliography of books for and about Puerto Ricans and other Latinos concludes the chapter.

CHAPTER 4. AFRICAN AMERICAN CHILDREN'S LITERATURE

This chapter is divided into three categories: (1) Contemporary Settings, (2) African American Traditions, and (3) African Americans to Remember. Books listed in the first category provide examples of contemporary life within African American culture. The second section concerns books that are adaptations of African and African American folktales or that give insight into traditions and customs of African Americans. The third section is an annotated bibliography of biographies and historical fiction.

CHAPTER 5. BOOKS FOR AND ABOUT CHINESE AMERICANS, JAPANESE AMERICANS, AND OTHER ASIAN AMERICANS

The first section focuses on children's books that accurately portray Chinese or Chinese American culture. The second section reviews the literature about Japanese Americans. The last section concentrates on books for or about Vietnamese Americans, Korean Americans, and other Asian Americans.

CHAPTER 6. BOOKS FOR AND ABOUT VARIOUS NATIVE AMERICANS

This chapter is divided into five sections: (1) Images of Native Americans, (2) Demographic Information, (3) Literature For and About Native Americans, (4) Historical Settings, and (5) Contemporary Settings. This chapter focuses on literature written for or about Native Americans. It provides an annotated bibliography of historical fiction and informational books about the various tribes of North America, as well as an annotated bibliography of titles focusing on contemporary life in the various tribes.

CHAPTER 7. ACTIVITIES FOR EXTENDING CHILDREN'S EXPERIENCES WITH MULTIETHNIC LITERATURE

The primary goal of this chapter is to provide adults with various hands-on activities that challenge students to expand their understanding of multiethnic literature. The activities are varied and adaptable to various age groups.

CHAPTER 8. CONCLUSIONS

This section focuses on the value of multiethnic children's literature in light of demographic trends in the United States.

APPENDIX. PUBLISHERS AND ADDRESSES

The appendix provides a listing of publishers' addresses to help adults locate titles listed in this book. Only those publishers with a title listed in this book are included in the appendix.

REFERENCES

Banks, J. A. (1992). It's up to us. *Teaching Tolerance, 1* (2), 20–23.

Acknowledgments

This book could not have been written without the help of several people who assisted us along the way. We would like to thank Becky Vickers from the Lubbock Christian University Library, who provided assistance when needed. Many students and colleagues provided articles and other material that they thought would be of benefit to us. A special thanks goes to Nellie Goad, library assistant for the Lamesa I.S.D., who always brought us the latest articles pertaining to multiethnic issues. We would also like to thank Dee Davis and Judith Holladay for their clerical assistance, and to the editors and staff at Delmar Publishers for their patience. Also, we want to express our appreciation to Russell Skiles of the *Lamesa Press Reporter* for allowing us to use several of his photographs. To our daughter María Elena goes a special thanks for her understanding when our time together was shortened during the writing of this book. To our recently adopted son, Victor Kiko we would like to thank him for giving us the renewed energy to complete this book.

For all the people too numerous to name who gave their support on this task *un abrazo fuerte* (a big hug)!

REVIEWERS

Frank D. Adams
Benedictine College

Tim Campbell
Southern Nazarene College

Linda S. Estes
Lindenwood Colleges

Denise Ann Finazzo
Edinburo University

Christine Flowers
Hillsdale College

Carol Lauritzen
Eastern Oregon State College

Hanfu Mi
Concord College

Wilma T. Robles
Nova University

Mary S. Rogers
University of Alabama

About the Authors

Gonzalo Ramirez is an elementary school principal at V.Z. Rogers Elementary School in the Lamesa Independent School District, Lamesa, Texas. He received a Doctor of Education degree in 1991 and a Master of Education degree in 1981 from Texas Tech University. His undergraduate degree is from Lubbock Christian University.

Dr. Ramirez taught graduate and undergraduate courses at Lubbock Christian University and Texas Tech University from 1983 to 1991. He conducts workshops and conference presentations on multicultural and effective school issues throughout the United States.

Jan Lee Ramirez is an elementary school principal at North Elementary School in the Lamesa Independent School District. She received a Master of Education degree from Texas Tech University in 1981 and a Bachelor of Education degree from Lubbock Christian University in 1977.

Mrs. Ramirez has been an elementary school teacher, Chapter 1 consultant, and an assistant principal. She conducts workshops and conference presentations on multicultural, parental involvement, and effective school topics. She is a member of numerous professional organizations.

Dedication

For our daughter of color, María Elena,
our newest child of color, Victor Kiko,
and all the children who have touched my life.

G.R.

Dedicated to our darling daughter, María Elena, who
loves to read books of and about various cultures,
and Victor Kiko, who is enjoying these same stories.

J.L.R.

WHY MULTIETHNIC CHILDREN'S LITERATURE? AN OVERVIEW

DEFINITION

Multiethnic children's literature is children's literature for and about America's four major nonwhite populations—Latinos (Americans of Mexican, Puerto Rican, Cuban, or other Hispanic American ancestry), African Americans (Americans of African ancestry who are not of Hispanic origin), Asian Americans (Americans of Japanese, Vietnamese, Chinese, Filipino, or other Asian ancestry) and Native Americans (members of American Indian tribes such as the Apache, Crow, Cherokee, Sioux, Blackfeet, and others). These four major nonwhite populations, referred to collectively as America's *people of color*, will lead the shift from a predominately white population to one that is nonwhite in the coming decades (González, 1990).

AMERICA'S RACIAL AND ETHNIC DIVERSITY

This is not to say that America's people of color are a monolithic community. The minority or culturally different populations within our borders have cultural, linguistic, and racial differences. Current trends show African Americans, Asian Americans, Latinos, and Native Americans composing the majority of the school-age population in the United States by the next century. Today, these four groups of children already make up the majority in many urban schools (Miller-Lachmann, 1992).

Over a relatively short period of time, we have dramatically changed the racial and ethnic makeup of our country, and all evidence suggests that this trend will continue into the next century. Of greater significance to educators is the anticipated increase in school-aged children of color from 25 percent in 1980 to 42 percent by the year 2000 (CMPEAL, 1988).

FIGURE 1-1 Children of color will be the majority in the next decade. Courtesy of Russell Skiles, Lamesa Press Reporter.

Because of the changing demographics of the United States and Canada over the past several decades, America's people of color have been able to participate more fully in the "American experience." Gone are the days of America's melting pot. Price (1992) states that the melting pot only works in some aspects of American life, and it seldom works socially. He argues that "it took decades of political, judicial, and legislative pressure to include . . . minorities" (p. 212).

Usher in the days of the "tossed salad!" Like the salad whose various ingredients make their individual contributions, America's culturally diverse populations, too, have made their individual contributions to the United States. Unfortunately, many of these groups are not mentioned in our history books.

Another factor to consider is the fact that not all of America's immigrants blended into one culture. Rather, some of our racial and ethnic groups preserved many of their own cultural traditions and lifestyles. For example, many Mexican Americans continue to celebrate Mexico's two independence days *Cinco de mayo* and *Diesiséis de septiembre*; Vietnamese Americans may celebrate *Thanh-Minh* and Chinese Americans may observe *Ching Ming*, two holidays reserved to honor one's ancestors; and various Asian American groups celebrate the new year in the spring by observing the Lunar New Year.

The United States is a multiethnic nation (Hernández, 1989). We are what we are as a nation because of the unique contributions that every racial and ethnic group has made to our way of life. Still, all Americans are not aware of many of the contributions of Mexican Americans, Chinese Americans, African Americans, Vietnamese Americans, and other people of color.

MULTICULTURAL OR MULTIETHNIC EDUCATION

Most dictionaries define *multiethnic education* as the study of large groups of different people who speak the same language, have the same beliefs and values, and come from the same national or racial group. For example, Chinese Americans are considered an American ethnic group because they tend to have common beliefs and customs that are similar to those of China's population while identifying with American culture to varying degrees.

As we see it, the term *multicultural* has a broader meaning than multiethnic. Multicultural education, for example, is the study of all peoples. A multicultural curriculum would provide insight into different people by teaching about the religious, racial, or social group to which they belong. Along with the study of African Americans, Latinos, Asian Americans, and Native Americans, knowledge about white ethnic groups such as Jewish Americans, Italian Americans, and others would also be included. The concept of multicultural education can also be expanded to include the study of people in other parts of the world.

Multicultural education is a vital part of any curriculum because the world is becoming more and more accessible to our children every day. As improvements in travel and telecommunications "shrink" our world, the need for children to understand the peoples of the world takes on greater importance. For the purpose of this book, we have decided to focus on literature for and about the four major nonwhite groups in the United States, or America's people of color. By focusing on these four groups, we feel that we are providing the children of America with a starting point for learning about and accepting people different from themselves.

RACIAL AND ETHNIC DIVERSITY IN CHILDREN'S LITERATURE

Children's literature that reflects the contributions, lifestyles, and values of these ethnic groups will help children to have a better understanding of who they are and what contributions they can make to this country (Martínez & Nash, 1990). This type of literature will benefit white children by helping them appreciate and understand America's various racial and ethnic groups. Literature can play an important part in helping all children learn about new worlds, new ideas, and different ways of doing things, which will benefit them as human beings (Rasinski & Padak, 1990).

The number of excellent books reflecting the culture, heritage, and contemporary experiences of America's people of color is small, but the opportunity nevertheless exists to use this type of literature to examine and respond to different cultural values and beliefs. This text will discuss some of these titles.

For example, Norah A. Dooley's *Everybody Cooks Rice* (1991) introduces readers to various cultures. The character, a young child, travels through his neighborhood looking for a family member. The boy sees that each household, in satisfying the basic human need for food, cooks rice differently depending on its culture.

We are well aware of the fact that different cultural and national identities exist within the various ethnic heritages. Reimer (1992) emphasizes this by stating that caution must be exercised when using children's literature to make sure that these different cultures are not lumped together into "cultural conglomerates." The example she provides is the use of the term *Hispanic* to mean any Latin American culture. Although we agree in principal with Reimer, we use the term *Latino* to organize the children's literature titles that best address the needs and reflect the culture of America's various Spanish-speaking people. For example, by organizing books within the category of Latino Children's Literature, we can evaluate and recommend appropriate titles

FIGURE 1-2 Minimizing the differences between the home and school life of our culturally different children should be a major goal of every school. Courtesy of Russell Skiles, Lamesa Press Reporter.

while focusing on particular Latino cultures. This is also true for literature for and about Asian Americans and Native American people.

VALUE OF MULTIETHNIC CHILDREN'S LITERATURE

Maxim (1989) suggests that one of the methods of enhancing the self-esteem of children is by respecting children and their culture. Culture plays an important part in the development of children's sense of self and self-esteem. Minimizing the differences between the home and school life of culturally different children is a major step in helping them experience success in school (Knapp & Shields, 1990). Incorporating the experiences of these children into the syllabus (actually or vicariously) brings their home and community life into the classroom.

Since culture plays such an important role in the evolution of a child's self, multiethnic children's books are essential if educators or caretakers are to minimize the differences between the home life of children of color and the schools they attend. Violet Harris, a professor at the University of Illinois at Urbana-Champaign, expresses this point of view as follows:

Children of color—African, Asian, Hispanic, and Native American—need multicultural literature. The inclusion of multicultural literature in schooling can affirm and empower these children and their culture. . . . Children can derive pleasure and pride from hearing and reading . . . and seeing illustrations of characters who look as if they stepped out of their homes and communities (Martínez & Nash, 1990 p. 599).

Multiethnic children's books allow teachers and other adults to become familiar with the cultural backgrounds of their students. For example, Marjorie Thayer and Elizabeth Emmanuel's *Climbing Sun: The Story of a Hopi Indian Boy* (1980) can enlighten teachers about less obvious aspects of Hopi culture, such as one-on-one teaching and learning through cooperative activities, which may not be emphasized in the school's culture. Within the school setting, the cultures of various groups can be shared through the use of other multiethnic titles. Unfortunately, only five to eight percent of the 5,000 children's books published annually are considered multiethnic (Martínez & Nash, 1990). Why are there so few books for America's children of color when their numbers are increasing? In order to understand the lack of this type of literature, a short history of multiethnic children's literature is useful.

HISTORY OF MULTIETHNIC CHILDREN'S LITERATURE

Multiethnic Children's Literature: the 1940s to the Mid-1970s

Multiethnic children's literature is a relatively new genre of children's literature when compared to the history of children's literature as a whole. In response to the criticism by some Americans of books that depicted people of color in terms of stereotypes or degrading roles, an attempt was made in the 1940s to write and publish multiethnic children's books. *Bright April* (1946) by Marguerite de Angeli, was one of the first books to deal with race issues and to have a positive nonwhite character. April Bright, sometimes referred to as Bright April, is an African American girl who must deal with racism in her Brownie Scout troop. Cullinan (1989) observes that by today's standards, *Bright April* (with its illustrations of African Americans with Caucasian features) would be considered a weak multiethnic book; it is nevertheless noteworthy because it was one of the first books to integrate African American and white characters.

In the 1960s and early 1970s, other children's books with African American characters continued the theme of pleading for understanding found in *Bright April*. Because of this underlying theme, Sims (1983) labeled these books "social conscience books." They usually involved one of the following plots: (1) an African American child moves into an all-white school, (2) an African American family moves into an all-white neighborhood, (3) African Americans fight discrimination using lawful methods such as petitions and nonviolent protests, or (4) African Americans learn to get along with whites (Sims, 1983).

What about other ethnic characters in children's books during this period? Books written about Mexican Americans (even fewer in number) also tended to be written with the aim of helping white (majority) children to sympathize with, empathize with, and tolerate Mexican Americans (Wagoner, 1982). Mexican American characters mostly displayed traditional Mexican male-female roles and lived in rural or impoverished circumstances. Education was stressed as the vehicle of advancement. Also, the Spanish language was not consistently used in these books (Wagoner, 1982).

In 1976, the Asian American Children's Book Project under the auspices of the Council on Interracial Books for Children reviewed children's books written between 1945 and 1975 in which one or more of the characters are Chinese American, Japanese American, or of another Asian American group. A total of 66 Asian American children's literature books were located. The committee found that most of the books portrayed Asian American characters as all looking alike and huddled together in Little Tokyos or Chinatowns (Aoki, 1981).

During the same time period, Native Americans also did not fare well in books depicting their contemporary culture. Gilliland (1982), in attempting to locate books about Native Americans to use with Northern Cheyenne children in the late 1960s, found very few books that "could help the Indian children build an accurate self-concept, or help non-Indian children accept their Indian neighbors as friends and equals" (p. 913). Most of these books depicted the Native Americans as savages or childlike.

Multiethnic Children's Literature: 1970s to the Present

Whereas most of the early multiethnic books mirrored the social issues of the time, the vast majority of the books published from the mid-1970s to the present have themes that are common to all realistic fiction.* Although these books were intended primarily for children of color, they offer a more universal message that white children are able to relate to the experiences of the characters. Sims (1983), in analyzing the history of African American children's literature, refers to these books as "culturally conscious."

The basic themes in the culturally conscious books reviewed by Sims involve at least one of the following: (1) heritage, (2) the battle against racism and discrimination, (3) everyday experiences, (4) urban living, (5) friendship, (6) family relationships, and (7) growing up. Although Sims surveyed only African American literature, many of these themes are also present in multiethnic titles written for Mexican Americans, Chinese Americans, Puerto Ricans, and others.

These books, many of which were written by people of color, provide an insider's point of view in that they provide a cultural context for a character's actions or thoughts. For example, Michele Maria Surat's book *Angel Child, Dragon Child* (1983) incorporates several of the themes described by Sims. Nguyen Hoa is a Vietnamese girl who is adapting to her new surroundings in the United States. The differences between school and everyday life in Vietnam and in the United States are confusing to this small child. Surat provides the reader with a vivid account of what it feels like to be different and at times rejected.

Melting-Pot Books: 1940 to the Present

Books that span both eras are those with illustrations that show people of color, but that address no racial issues. These books are referred to as *melting-pot books* because they suggest that Americans are a homogeneous group sharing the same lifestyle (Sims, 1983). In these books, characters from different ethnic and racial backgrounds are devoid of any cultural characteristics except for superficial traits (Miller-Lachmann, 1992).

For example, a melting-pot book with a Latino protagonist is Matt Christopher's *Centerfield Ballhawk* (1992). Christopher is a noted author of children's sport stories. *Centerfield Ballhawk* is the story of José Méndez, the son of a former minor-league ballplayer who is afraid his low batting average will disappoint his father. This very entertaining story does not provide any cultural information about the Latino culture of the Méndez family.

---

* The difference is that most recent titles while focusing on themes of interest to all children (such as acceptance by peers, love, and becoming independent), have main characters who are Latinos, African Americans, Asian Americans, or Native Americans.

Two examples of other recently published melting-pot books are Allen Say's *A River Dream* (1988) and *The Lost Lake* (1989). In *A River Dream*, a young boy lying in bed with a fever opens a gift from his Uncle Scott. Mayflies fly out the window and his neighborhood is transformed into a forest with a river. He takes a rowboat down the river and meets his Uncle Scott. The text and illustrations depict Mark and Uncle Scott as Asian Americans in an attractive, realistic, and contemporary middle-class setting. However, they do not help to identify them as Chinese Americans, Japanese Americans, or as members of another Asian American group.

The Lost Lake is a story in which a young boy named Luke goes to spend the summer with his father. The text provides no information to give the reader insight into a specific culture. Say's realistic drawings show a boy and his father—both with Asian features. Luke's dad is an architect or draftsman. Other middle-class characteristics are found throughout the story—the story depicts a modest home, Luke's brand-new hiking boots, and a week of backpacking in the mountains.

These three stories exemplify the positive aspects of multiethnic children's literature. Melting-pot books such as *Centerfield Ballhawk, A River Dream*, and *The Lost Lake* do not depict their culturally different characters in a stereotyped or degrading way. These books tend to highlight our similarities as North Americans regardless of racial or ethnic affiliation (Miller-Lachmann, 1992). Sims (1983) would argue that a major flaw of melting-pot books is that they deny the existence of distinctive cultural heritages by suggesting that all Americans, regardless of race or ethnicity, share the same middle-class experiences and values. According to Chu and Schuler (1992), the omission of references of cultural traits could be viewed as positive in that all Americans regardless of cultural or racial heritage are Americans first. But these authors do stress that new immigrants to our country need to see their culture reflected in our literature. We would argue that second and third generations of racially and culturally different American children also need to identify with characters of the same heritage.

Nonetheless, this group of books have made an historical contribution to multiethnic children's literature by allowing mainstream America to see people of color as a part of America, and by allowing the children of people of color to see themselves in the literature. Also, melting-pot books often show people of color in middle-class settings, which helps to counteract stereotyped images of many people of color. Our suggestion is that melting-pot books be used along with other books that provide more insight into specific cultures.

FIGURE 1-3 Learning about cultures different from their own will help children understand each other. Courtesy of Russell Skiles, Lamesa Press Reporter.

QUANTITY OF MULTIETHNIC CHILDREN'S LITERATURE

When we look at the history of multiethnic children's literature, we notice that one of the obvious problems is the limited number of books for and about America's people of color. Larrick (1965) wrote an article in the *Saturday Review* about her research on African American children's literature published between 1962 and 1964. Of the 5,206 children's books published during this period, only 6.7 percent included at least one African American in the illustrations or text.

Chall et al. (1979) duplicated Larrick's study and found that 14.4 percent of the 4,775 children's books published between 1973 and 1975 included at least one African American character in the illustrations or text. This increase proved to be short-lived. By the 1980s, about one percent of the children's books published were about African Americans (Bishop, 1987). How did other people of color fare during this same period?

FUTURE IMPLICATIONS FOR MULTIETHNIC CHILDREN'S LITERATURE

Larrick's, Chall's, and Bishop's research focused on the portrayal of African Americans in children's literature, but the limited exposure of other people of color is also quite evident, though not as well-documented (Reimer, 1992). With one percent of the children's books published depicting African Americans, even fewer books dealt with other culturally different groups (Bishop, 1987).

Bishop (1991) sees the 1990s as the decade of renewed interest in books about African Americans. In contrast, Swanson (1992) states that of the 5,000 children's books published in 1992, only 51 were written and or illustrated by African American authors, and fewer were created by authors of other culturally different groups. While a few of the small presses that published multiethnic children's literature during the lean years, such as Children's Book Press in San Francisco and Mariposa Publishing in Santa Fe, New Mexico, continue to publish folktales and picture books about Mexican Americans, Japanese Americans, Native Americans, and others, many had closed by the 1980s (Miller-Lachmann, 1992). These small presses, which also printed many materials in bilingual formats (English and native languages), provided positive images for children of color.

We must address the lack of multiethnic children's literature if children's literature is to provide an opportunity for children to learn about the culture and history of North America's culturally different people. Ways of increasing the number of books reflecting our cultural diversity must be found. To begin with, major publishing presses must give authors outside of mainstream America an opportunity to grow and mature with each manuscript, rather than offering them only "one time shots."

Another possibility is for state education agencies and school districts to force publishers to provide books that reflect the cultural diversity within our schools. Also, small publishing houses (such as Cinco Puntos Press in El Paso, Texas, Arte Público Press in Houston, Texas, and Trails West Publishing, in Santa Fe, New Mexico) that are producing multiethnic children's literature must be supported and given an opportunity to sell their books to our schools and public libraries.

LOCATING MULTIETHNIC CHILDREN'S LITERATURE

It may be argued that a book on multiethnic children's literature is not needed, because many major and small publishing houses now offer their own annotated multiethnic literature bibliographies. We would remind our readers that the reason publishers publish books is to sell them and make a profit. While we support the free enterprise system, we feel that publishing houses should not be the sole evaluators of multiethnic children's literature.

For example, while researching this book, we came across a publisher's multiethnic bibliography that included Claire H. Bishop and Kurt Wiese's *The Five Chinese Brothers* (1938), a simple story of four brothers who cleverly save the "First Chinese Brother" from being executed. Although the story may be appealing because the brothers use such creative methods to solve their problem, the book is not an example of good multiethnic children's literature because it reinforces the idea that all Asians look alike. Of course, the five brothers may be quintuplets but all the people assembled on the village square also look alike!

We would also like to point out that some of the books written before 1980 may not be available in some school and public libraries, since some of these titles were allowed to go out of print. Rollock (1984) noticed that many of the African American titles listed in her 1979 book, *The Black Experience in Children's Books*, were no longer being published in 1984. If we are to give children an opportunity to experience cultural diversity through literature, we must seek out some of these books. One way is through the interlibrary loan program in which most public and university libraries participate. Books that are not on the shelves of your library may be requested through this program, which allows your library to ask other public and university libraries for a copy of the book you desire.

By selecting the titles mentioned in this book, you will be providing your children with the information they need to function in our

FIGURE 1-4 Children need to acknowledge diversity in order to function in our diverse society. Courtesy of Russell Skiles, Lamesa Press Reporter.

pluralistic society. Every effort should be made to incorporate multiethnic children's literature into every public library, school library, and classroom, regardless of the racial makeup of the school. By doing so, we will be that much closer to becoming a society that acknowledges its diversity and that lives in harmony as a result.

With over 5,000 children's books published annually, teachers, librarians, caretakers, and other adults need to continually seek new multiethnic titles. The following are two sets of recommended materials. The first is a list of professional resources that will aid adults interested in locating and selecting high-quality multiethnic children's literature. A brief description of each book is provided.

The second bibliography contains review journals that may also assist adults in locating new multiethnic titles. Articles and reviews of children's and juvenile books for or about African Americans, Latinos, Asian Americans, and Native Americans frequently appear in these journals. Using these resources will allow adults to provide children with the opportunity to better appreciate and understand the contributions and variety of the culturally different people of the United States.

Professional Resources

Freeman, Yvonne S. & Cervantes, Carolina. (1991). *Literature Books en Español for Whole Language: An Annotated Bibliography.* Tucson, AZ: University of Arizona, College of Education, Program in Language and Literacy, Division of Language, Reading, and Culture.

An annotated bibliography of recently published books in Spanish from the United States, Mexico, South America, and Spain (written in English).

Hirschfelder, A. B. (1982). *American Indian Stereotypes in the World of Children: A Reader and Biography.* Metuchen, NJ: Scarecrow Press.

Provides valuable information on children's perceptions of Native Americans. A list of recommended materials is included.

Jenkins, E. C. & Austin, M. C. (1987). *Literature for Children About Asians and Asian American: Analysis and Annotated Bibliography, With Additional Readings for Adults.* Westport, CT: Greenwood Press.

Books for and about Chinese Americans, Japanese Americans, Korean Americans, and other Asian Americans are listed in this annotated bibliography.

Kruse, Ginny M. & Horning, Kathleen T. (1991). *Multicultural Literature for Children and Young Adults: A Selected Listing of*

Books 1980-1990 By and About People of Color, (3rd ed). Madison, WI: Cooperative Children's Book Center.

Books appropriate for preschool through young adult are listed in this annotated bibliography of books for and about African Americans, Asian Americans, Hispanic Americans, and Native Americans .

Lima, Carolyn W. (1989). *A to Zoo: Subject Access to Children's Books*. New York: R. R. Bowker.

A list of picture books for and about different ethnic groups in the United States is listed in one of the chapters.

Miller-Lachmann, L. (ed.). (1992). *Our Family, our Friends, Our World: An Annotated Guide to Significant Multicultural Books for Children and Teenagers*. New York: R. R. Bowker.

The first four chapters provide an annotated list of multiethnic English language titles for and about African Americans, Asian Americans, Hispanic Americans, and Native Americans.

The Native American Authors Distribution Project. (1992). Greenfield Center, NY: The Greenfield Review Press.

More than 250 titles by authors of American Indian ancestry are included in this small catalogue. Publications include children's and adult books.

Rollock, Barbara. (ed). (1989). *The Black Experience in Children's Books*. New York: New York Public Library.

Divided by age group, this is an annotated bibliography of books intended for African American children.

Rudman, M. K. (1984). *Children's Literature: An Issues Approach*, (2nd ed.). New York: Longman.

Chapter 5 (Heritage) focuses on discussion and books for and about Native Americans, African Americans, Hispanic Americans, and Asian Americans.

Schon, Isabel. (1988). *A Hispanic Heritage: A Guide to Juvenile Books About Hispanic People and Culture*, (3rd ed.). Metuchen, NJ: Scarecrow Press.

An annotated bibliography of books in English from Spanish-speaking countries of the world.

Slapin, B., and Seale, D. (1988). *Books Without Bias: Through Indian Eyes*. Berkeley, CA: Oyate Press.

Guidelines for selecting books for and about Native Americans are included in this book, which focuses on discussion of Native American issues. An extensive annotated list is also provided.

Review Journals

Booklinks. Chicago, IL: American Library Association.

Booklist. Chicago, IL: American Library Association.

Bulletin of the Center for Children's Books. Chicago: The University of Chicago Press.

The Hornbook Magazine. Boston, MA: Hornbook.

Interracial Books for Children Bulletin. New York: Council on Interracial Books for Children.

Language Arts. Urbana, IL.: National Council of Teachers of English.

The Reading Teacher. Newark, DE: International Reading Association.

School Library Journal. Marion, OH: Bowker.

REFERENCES

Aoki, E. M. (1981). Are you Chinese? Are you Japanese? Or are you just a mixed-up kid? Using Asian American children's literature. *The Reading Teacher, 34,* 382-385.

Bishop, C. H., and Wiese, K. (1938). *The Five Chinese Brothers.* New York: Coward-McCann.

Bishop, R. S. (1987). Extending multicultural understanding through children's books. In B. Cullinan (ed.), *Children's Literature in the Reading Program* (pp. 60-67). Newark, DE: International Reading Association.

Bishop, R. S. (1991). African American literature for today's children: Anchor, compass, and sail. *Perspectives, 7,* ix-xii.

Chall, J. S., Radwin, E., French, V. W., & Hall, C.R. (1979) Blacks in the world of children's books. *The Reading Teacher, 32,* 527-533.

Chu, E. & Schuler, C. V. (1992). United States: Asian Americans. In Miller-Lachmann, L. (ed.), *Our Family, Our Friends, Our World: An Annotated Guide to Significant Multicultural Books for Children and Teenagers.* New York: R. R. Bowker.

Commission of Minority Participation in Education and American Life (CMPEAL). (1988). One third of a nation. Washington:

CMPEAL. In González, R. D. (1990). When minority becomes majority: The changing face of English classrooms. *English Journal, 79,* 16-23.

Cullinan, B. E. (1989). *Literature and the Child,* (2nd ed.). New York: Harcourt Brace Jovanavich.

de Angeli, M. (1946). *Bright April.* Garden City, NY: Doubleday & Company.

Dooley, N. A. (1991). *Everybody Cooks Rice.* Minneapolis: Carolrhoda Books.

Gilliland, H. (1982). The new view of Native Americans in children's books. *The Reading Teacher, 35,* 912-916.

González, R. D. (1990). When minority becomes majority: The changing face of English classrooms. *English Journal, 79,* 16-23.

Hernández, H. (1989). *Multicultural Education: A Teacher's Guide to Content and Process.* Columbus, OH: Merrill Publishing Company.

Knapp, M. S., & Shields, P.M. (1990). Reconceiving academic instruction for the children in poverty. *Phi Delta Kappa, 71,* 752-758.

Larrick, N. (1965, September). The all-white world of children's books. *Saturday Review,* pp. 63-65, 84-85.

Miller-Lachmann, L. (ed.). (1992). *Our Family, Our Friends, Our World: An Annotated Guide to Significant Multicultural Books for Children and Teenagers.* New York: R. R. Bowker.

Martínez, M. & Nash, M. F. (1990). Bookalogues: Talking about children's literature. *Language Arts, 67,* 599-606.

Maxim, G. (1989). *The Very Young: Guiding Children From Infancy Through the Early Years,* (3rd ed.). Columbus, OH: Merrill Publishing Company.

Price, H. B. (1992). Multiculturalism: Myths and realities. *Phi Delta Kappa, 74,* 208-213.

Rasinski, T. & Padak, N. D. (1990). Multicultural learning through children's literature. *Language Arts, 67,* 576-580.

Reimer, K. M. (1992). Multiethnic literature: Holding fast to dreams. *Language Arts, 69,* 14-20.

Rollock, B. (1984). *The Black Experience in Children's Books,* (2nd ed.). New York: New York Public Library.

Say, A. (1988). *A River Dream.* New York: Houghton Mifflin Company.

Say, A. (1989). *The Lost Lake.* New York: Houghton Mifflin Company.

Sims, R. (1983). What has happened to the "all-white" world of children's books? *Phi Delta Kappa, 64,* 650-653.

Surat M. M. (1983). *Angel Child, Dragon Child.* New York: Scholastic.

Swanson, B. (1992, April). *Spice Up the Melting Pot: What's New in Multicultural Literature, Grades 4-8.* Paper presented at the 1992 Texas State Reading Association Conference, El Paso, TX.

Thayer, M. & Emmanuel, E. (1980). *Climbing Sun: The Story of a Hopi Indian Boy.* New York: Dodd, Mead and Company.

Wagoner, S. A. (1982). Mexican Americans in children's literature since 1970. *The Reading Teacher, 36,* 274-279.

2 GUIDELINES FOR SELECTING MULTIETHNIC LITERATURE

Lattimer (1976) stated that white children are given a misrepresented view of American society. In television, movies, and literature, the pluralistic nature of the United States is still not valued. Although advances have been made in children's literature in including members of different racial, ethnic, and linguistic groups, there are still only a small number of books from which to choose.

Swanson (1992) states that only 51 out of the 5,000 books written in 1991 were written by African Americans and fewer still by other people of color. With so few books about people of color and even fewer written by people of color, an effort must be made by teachers and others to see that high-quality multiethnic children's literature is incorporated into the curricula of our schools and into our libraries. Multiethnic children's books must meet certain criteria if they are to provide a positive and accurate representation of an ethnic or racial group (Cullinan, 1989). What are the criteria that "good" multiethnic children's literature must meet?

LITERARY ELEMENTS

To begin with, multiethnic children's literature must be evaluated using the same standards by which any other type of literature is evaluated. A multiethnic children's book may teach children to respect their culture or to respect the culture of others, but unless the book continues to hold their attention after they have picked it up, education in this area will not take place. The literary elements of *plot, characterization, setting, style, theme,* and *point of view* are interwoven to provide an interesting story. These literary elements are also important considerations when evaluating a multiethnic book.

Plot

How an author uses action, conflict, and resolution of the conflict as parts of the plot is important in creating a vicarious multiethnic experience. Finding out what happens next is very important to children (Cullinan,1989). For example, Nancy Van Loan's *El Dorado* (1991), a folktale from Colombia, tells the story of a queen and her daughter who leave the king one night to live in the palace of an emerald serpent in Lake Guatavita. With the conflict well developed through a chain of events that has the queen and princess happy in the serpent's palace but the king longing for his family, the reader is eager to learn the ending. Van Loan's *El Dorado*, through its well-written text and beautiful illustrations, likewise provides a plot whose action develops naturally and entertainingly.

Characterization

How an author develops the characters is also of importance. The characters should be developed in the course of the story so that children are able to relate to them. In multiethnic children's literature,

FIGURE 2-1 *Annie and the Old One* by Miska Miles. Copyright © 1971 by Little, Brown and Company (Inc.). Reprinted by permission of Little, Brown and Company.

this is crucial if the reader is to discover the similarities and differences between cultures. An author provides readers with "cultural representatives" by creating well-developed ethnic characters.

For example, in Miska Miles' *Annie and the Old One* (1971), children who have a beloved older family member will understand the young Navaho girl's anguish when she learns that her grandmother is going to die. They will feel Annie's desperation and anguish as she attempts to keep her grandmother from leaving and returning to Mother Earth. How Annie finally accepts her grandmother's death is made clear through the words of the author, who has made Annie likeable and believable. Although fictional, Annie's character becomes real as she learns to make adjustments in her life after the death of her grandmother.

Setting

The setting of a story provides the reader or listener with a context for the story in terms of time frame and place. The setting of a multiethnic book is important because it can provide children with additional geographic and cultural information. Bryd Baylor's books, such as *The Desert Is Theirs* (1975), *Hawk, I'm Your Brother* (1976), and *The Other Way To Listen* (1978), provide children with opportunities to see how the mountains, deserts, wildflowers, and other living things continue to be integral parts of the lives of the various American Indian tribes of the Southwest and the Great Plains.

Author's Style

The words the author uses to tell a multiethnic story are very important. By selecting specific words, an author can help the reader gain a better understanding of an ethnic character or a culturally different setting. The author may also be able to provide a new perspective on a common setting or situation by presenting it through the eyes of an ethnic character. For example, in Elizabeth F. Howard's *Aunt Flossie's Hats (and Crab Cakes Later)* (1991), a Sunday afternoon visit to Aunt Flossie's house is a special treat for two African American girls because they are allowed to look through Aunt Flossie's hatboxes. As the girls and Aunt Flossie drink tea and eat cookies, Aunt Flossie recounts the times she wore each hat. Howard communicates Aunt Flossie's memories through the rhythmic use of simple words.

Theme

Themes of love, courage, friendship, and sacrifice, to name a few, are as common in multiethnic literature as they are in any other type of literature. A universal theme, such as coping with the loss of a parent in Lucille Clifton's *Everett Anderson's Goodbye* (1983), helps children see that struggles such as those of Everett, an African American child, could be the struggles of any child.

However, because America's people of color have had particular experiences, multiethnic children's literature contains additional themes. For example, the universal theme of love is present in Camille Yarbrough's *Cornrows* (1979), but the additional theme of learning about and developing pride in one's heritage is developed through the telling of the history of the braided hairstyle called "cornrows." Throughout the story of a young girl and her extended family, African and African American history and culture are shared with the reader.

Point of View

Although point of view may not be considered a crucial element in the telling of a story, an author's choice of the first-person point of view (i.e., "I am going to tell you what happened to me in my neighborhood") or the third-person point of view (i.e., "He was sitting in the living room watching television") can determine how effectively a story is told. In multiethnic children's literature this is important because an author's choice to use the first-person point of view will provide us with the thoughts of the culturally different person, while the third-person point of view may provide us with more of an outsider's perspective on the characters and story. The reader and writer both need to answer the question, "Is the main character more of a participant or an observer?"

FURTHER EVALUATION OF MULTIETHNIC LITERATURE

Multiethnic children's books must have an appropriate plot, characterization, setting, style, theme, and point of view if they are to be of interest to children. For multiethnic children's literature to be considered worthwhile, other criteria must be met as well.

Using a Second Language

Since language is an important aspect of culture, some multiethnic books written in English will include non-English words in the text. Therefore, we must emphasize the following point: correct pronunciation of non-English names and words is essential to show respect for the culture.

Adults may be hesitant to use multiethnic literature because they feel inadequate about pronouncing the non-English words. However, we have a special responsibility to share this type of literature with our children in order to broaden their horizons and let our children of color see themselves in literature. Our advice to adults who do not know the language found in these books is to use a resource person. For example, Mexican American children or parents for whom Spanish is a first or second language could be utilized as resource people for Gary Soto's *Taking Sides* (1991), Soto uses Spanish words and phrases throughout this book to provide realism since the main character,

Lincoln Mendoza, has grown up in a Mexican American neighborhood.

Some books provide a pronunciation key for non-English words used in the story. Books such as Michele M. Surat's *Angel Child, Dragon Child* (1983) provide a pronunciation key at the bottom of the page or in the form of a glossary. By providing help with the pronunciation of such words as *Quang* (pronounced kwang), *chao buoi sang* (chow bwee sung), and other Vietnamese words, the book adds to the authenticity of the culture represented in the story.

These books allow our children of color to affirm the value of their non-English language and develop strong self-esteem (Radencich, 1985). This was made clear to me when teaching fourth grade reading to my class of 27 students that included one Latino student who could not read in English. With limited materials written in Spanish, my student and I spent the day attempting to learn and teach English as best we could at the time. Shortly thereafter, I brought to school a copy of Margot C. Griego's *Tortillitas para mama* (1981), a Spanish/English collection of Mexican nursery rhymes, to use with the entire class. As my Latino student began to read the Spanish versions to the rhymes with ease, I could see his confidence grow with every rhyme.

Other Issues to Consider

It is also important to evaluate the story and the roles of the characters before accepting a book as worthwhile multiethnic children's literature. Is the portrayal of characters accurate, and does the story reflect the culture realistically? The following selection guidelines, derived from the recommendations of the Asian American Children's Book Project Committee (1976), Little Soldier (1989), Schon (1983), and Swanson (1992), will help teachers, caretakers, and other adults who work with children select appropriate titles for and about people from all ethnic backgrounds. These basic guidelines suggest that multiethnic children's books should:

1. Contain text that reflects an authentic and sincere portrayal of the way of life of the group portrayed.

2. Attempt to amend historical errors and omissions by providing accurate information about people from the group portrayed who have made contributions to the United States and the world.

3. Replace prejudiced descriptions and stereotyped characters with ones that are more true to life and provide positive images.

4. Contain illustrations and/or photos that provide a true reflection of the way of life of the group.

5. Depict women of the group in transition from more traditional to more contemporary roles under the influence of the culture of their new homes in America.

6. Contain language that provides insight into the culture of the group.

CONCLUSION

Using these criteria to evaluate multiethnic children's books is important as more books about children of color reach our schools and public libraries. The multiethnic children's books mentioned in Chapter 3, Books For and About Mexican Americans, Puerto Ricans, and Other Latinos; in Chapter 4, Books For and About African Americans; in Chapter 5, Books For and About Chinese Americans, Japanese Americans, and Other Asian Americans; and in Chapter 6, Books For and About Various Native Americans are considered by many to be appropriate titles depicting the experiences of people of color in the United States.

Chapter 7, Activities for Extending Children's Experiences with Multiethnic Literature provides suggestions for and examples of activities that will help children to participate more fully in cultural experiences introduced in of these books. Some of the books are not flawless, but they can be read aloud and most are suitable for individual use. Special notes are provided to help individuals use some of the titles with elementary school children.

REFERENCES

Asian American Children's Book Project Committee. (1976). Criteria for analyzing books on Asian Americans. *Interracial Books for Children Bulletin*, 7, 4-5.

Baylor, B. (1975). *The desert is theirs.* New York: Charles Scribner's Sons.

Baylor, B. (1976). *Hawk, I'm your brother.* New York: Charles Scribner's Sons.

Baylor, B. (1978). *The other way to listen.* New York: Charles Scribner's Sons.

Clifton, L. (1983). *Everett Anderson's goodbye.* New York: Henry Holt & Company.

Cullinan, B. E. (1989). *Literature and the child* (2nd ed.). New York: Harcourt Brace Jovanovich.

Griego, Margot C., Bucks, Betsy L., Gilbert, Sharon S., and Kimball, Laurel H. (1981). *Tortillitas para mama and other. nursery rhymes: Spanish and English.* New York: Holt, Rinehart and Winston, 1981.

Howard, E. F. (1991). *Aunt Flossie's hats (and crab cakes later)*. New York: Clarion Books.

Lattimer, B. L. (1976). Telegraphing messages to children about minorities. *The Reading Teacher, 30,* 151-156.

Little Soldier, L. (1989, November). *Teaching about Native Americans by using children's literature.* Paper presented at the 1989 National Association for the Education of Young Children Conference, Atlanta, GA.

Van Loan, N. (1991). *El Dorado.* New York: Alfred A. Knopf.

Miles, M. (1971). Annie and the Old One. Boston: Little, Brown and Company.

Radencich, M. C. (1985). Books that promote positive attitudes toward second language learning. *The Reading Teacher, 38,* 526-530.

Schon, I. (1983). Books in Spanish and bilingual books for young readers: Some good, some bad. *School Library Journal, 29,* 87-91.

Soto, G. (1991). *Taking sides.* New York: Harcourt Brace Jovanovich.

Surat, M. M. (1983). *Angel child, dragon child.* New York: Scholastic.

Swanson, B. (1992, April). *Spice up the melting pot: What's new in multicultural literature, grades 4-8.* Paper presented at the 1992 Texas State Reading Association Conference, El Paso, TX.

Yarbrough, C. (1979). *Cornrows.* New York: Coward-McCann.

BOOKS FOR AND ABOUT MEXICAN AMERICANS, PUERTO RICANS, AND OTHER LATINOS

LATINO VERSUS HISPANIC

Latino is a relatively new term that, in our opinion, provides a more precise classification for a specific group of people than the word *Hispanic*. Latino emphasizes the bond with the indigenous people of the Americas, while Hispanic asserts cultural unity with Spain. For many Latinos—the people in the United States whose cultural heritages are derived from the Spanish-speaking cultures of Mexico, Central America, South America, and the Caribbean—the Spanish language may be the only true cultural tie they have with Spain and the Spanish language spoken in the Americas is different from that spoken in Spain.

For example, several Mexican Indian words are used by Mexican Americans in place of the Spanish words. The words *guajolote* (turkey), *tecolote* (owl), and *cacahuate* (peanut) are used instead of the Spanish words *pavo*, *buho*, and *maní*.

We are well aware of the fact that different cultural and national differences exist within the various Latino heritages. Some books, such as *Extraordinary Hispanic Americans* describe various Latino cultures within the same book. This chapter will provide bibliographies and descriptions of books for and about Mexican Americans and Puerto Ricans because they are the two largest Spanish-speaking communities in the United States. Books about other Spanish-speaking communities, such as Colombian Americans and Nicaraguan Americans, will be discussed in the section Books for and About Other Latinos. Some of these books provide both Spanish and English text.

Since Mexican Americans, Puerto Ricans, and other Latino children may come to school with Spanish as a first or second language, the use of Spanish must be valued there. De Cortes (1992) states that Maria Hall Etts's *Bad Boy, Good Boy* (1967) is an example of the children's books written in the 1960s and 1970s about Spanish-speaking Americans whose message was that speaking Spanish interfered with one's ability to become a functioning member of American society. As our nation becomes more of a global partner in business, government, and other areas, Americans who speak two or more languages will be able to make a stronger contribution. Therefore, contemporary books about Latino children can help children from various backgrounds see the Spanish language as an asset rather than a liability.

In addition, Schon (1988) believes that the exposure Latino children receive to a wide variety of English-language as well as Spanish-language books is the key to producing lifelong readers. Our own experiences have shown us that exposing monolingual English-speaking children or other non-Spanish-speaking children to Spanish-language books can interest them in learning a second language. The possibilities of using books written with English/Spanish text with our children are exciting! Finally, these bilingual formats make it possible for both English and Spanish speakers to share the same book.

MEXICAN AMERICAN CHILDREN'S LITERATURE

According to the 1990 U.S. Census, Mexican Americans, with approximately 13.5 million people, make up 5.4 percent of the population. The 1980 numbers were 8.7 million, or 3.9 percent of the population, indicating that the Mexican American population increased by 4.8 million, or 1.5 percent in just ten years—an increase that makes them the fastest growing ethnic group in the United States.

Of those included in the "Hispanic origin" census category, this country saw an increase within the same ten-year period of about 8 million new Spanish-speaking people, or 2.6 percent. According to González (1992), about 52 percent of children of color in U.S. schools are from Spanish-speaking homes. Given this shift in demographics, what can we as teachers and librarians do to prepare for the educational future of our fastest growing ethnic group?

Statistically, Mexican Americans and other Latinos have not fared well in the American school system. González (1992) cites a report from the National Council of La Raza, which states that nearly 50 percent of Mexican Americans drop out before graduating from high school. We believe strongly that only when Mexican American and other Latino children are given an opportunity to learn through literature that speaks to them—stories that are filled with their culture and that celebrate the uniqueness of their culture—will we begin to see an educational system that does not fail these children.

De Cortes (1992) adds that children's book publishers along with teachers and librarians, can contribute to reducing the dropout rate of Mexican Americans by legitimizing their dual heritage through books. Publishers must be willing to give Latino authors, like other authors, an opportunity to grow with each new work.

Through literature, Latino children have an opportunity to see themselves both as part of a culture and as individuals. Given this opportunity, Latinos will become true learners (De Cortes, 1992). The following are titles that will provide Mexican American children with information about who they are and what the members of their community have accomplished.

Aardema, Verna. (1991). *Borreguita and the Coyote: Tale from Ayutla, Mexico*. New York: Alfred A. Knopf. Grades K-2.

Borreguita, which means little lamb, uses her wit to keep Coyote from eating her. Children will delight in seeing Borreguita save herself by tricking Coyote day after day. The beautiful illustrations by Petra Mathers add to the humor of the story. A glossary of five Spanish words used in the story is provided at the beginning of the story. Another noteworthy telling of a traditional Mexican tale by Aardema is *The Riddle of the Drum: A Tale from Tizapán, México* (1979, Four Winds).

Anaya, Rudolfo A. (1987). *The Farolitos of Christmas*. Santa Fe, NM: New Mexico Magazine. Grades K-2.

A possible explanation for the tradition of lighting *farolitos* or *luminarios* (paper sacks weighted with sand that hold a lit candle inside) on Christmas Eve to help Joseph and Mary find their way to shelter is given in this story. The colorful illustrations by Richard C. Sandoval help tell the story of a fourth grader's attempt to bring the traditional shepherd's play to her house. Since her grandfather is unable to help her light the bonfires needed, she designs the *farolitos* as a last-minute substitute. A good introduction to a Christmas tradition observed by many people of Mexican descent.

Atkinson, Mary. (1979). *María Teresa*. Carrboro, NC: Lollipop Power. Grades K-2.

María Teresa, a young girl from New Mexico, has moved to Ohio where her mother is to attend Ohio Western University. Life in Ohio is very different from life in New Mexico for Mari Tere, as she is called by family and friends. The teacher and students have a difficult time pronouncing her name, school is different, no Spanish books are to be found, and even the supermarket does not have the foods and spices to which she is accustomed. She shares her problems with her puppet *Monteja la Oveja* (Monteja the lamb), who only speaks Spanish. When Mari Tere brings Monteja to school one day, the puppet becomes a bridge that helps Mari Tere and the other children to better understand each other.

Beatty, Patricia. (1981). *Lupita Mañana*. New York: William Morrow and Company. Grades 6-8.

When Lupita's father dies, she and her brother Salvador travel to the United States as undocumented workers (be aware that "wetback" and "illegal alien" are offensive terms). This story reflects the immigrant experience as seen through the eyes of a 13-year-old girl who must go to work to help support her family in Mexico. The added burden of being in continuous fear of deportation is also a major part of their lives.

Behrens, June. (1978) *Fiesta: Cinco de Mayo*. Chicago: Children's Press. Grades 3-5.

Activities usually associated with the celebration of *Cinco de mayo* (5th of May), which is Mexico's day of independence from French occupation, are captured in this photo essay. Children will be able to understand the reasons for celebrating *Cinco de mayo* and understand the differences between *Cinco de mayo* and *Dieciséis de septiembre* (September 16th), the celebration that marks Mexico's independence from Spain.

Bethancourt, T. Ernesto. (1985). *The Me Inside of Me*. Minneapolis: Lerner Publications. Grades 6-8.

Alfredo Flores is left behind with a cold while his family goes to Mexico City to visit a dying aunt. When the airplane crashes, 17-year-old Alfredo is left alone. Since his mother was fearful of flying, she had taken out accident insurance shortly before the

FIGURE 3-1 *The Me Inside of Me* by T. Ernesto Bethancourt, copyright © 1985 by Tom Paisley, published by Lerner Publications, Minneapolis.

plane left California. Alfred must now learn to cope with life alone and with a new found fortune. Under the guardianship of an old family friend he is enrolled in a preparatory school so that he can be admitted to Stanford University the following year. The cultural shock that Alfredo experiences and his inability to fit into his new environment are made believable by the author's descriptions of Alfredo's feelings. The book will appeal to older Latino students able to relate to Alfredo's difficulties and triumphs.

Bruin, Mary Ann Smothers. (1985) *Rosita's Christmas Wish.* San Antonio, TX: TexArt Services, Inc. Grades 3-5.

Rosita, a young girl living in San Antonio, is excited about the Christmas season that is approaching. The reader will learn about traditional Mexican Christmas customs such as *las posadas*, a live reenactment of the Christmas story. Also, life in a predominately Mexican American neighborhood in San Antonio is shared with the reader.

Clendenen, Mary Joe. (1990). *Gonzalo: Coronado's Shepherd Boy.* Austin, TX: Eakin Press. Grades 6-8.

FIGURE 3-2 *Gonzalo: Coronado's Shepherd Boy* by Mary Joe Clendenen, copyright © 1990 by Eakin Press. Reprinted by permission of the author.

Set in the early 1500s, the story concerns 11-year-old Gonzalo, the son of a Spanish indentured servant and an Aztec woman. He pleads with his father, a sheepherder on General

Coronado's expedition to the southwest United States, to let him go on this expedition. Drawing on detailed research, Clendenin tells the story of Coronados' exploits through the eyes of one of the first *Mestizos*, people of Spanish and Native Indian ancestry. A 10-page glossary at the end provides definitions of Spanish and Indian words used in the story.

Clinton, Susan Maloney. (1990). *Everett Alvarez, Jr.: A Hero For Our Times*. Chicago: Children's Press. Grades 3-5.

When Everett Alvarez, Jr., an American pilot, was shot down over North Vietnam on August 5, 1964, he became the first American prisoner-of-war (POW). Before he was released in 1973, he had been tortured, starved, and isolated, as were other American POWs. This book tells how Alvarez's love for his family helped him survive to become the longest-held American POW. The black-and-white photographs of Alvarez as a child and of his family add an effective element to this story of a true American hero.

Codye, Corinn. (1991). *Vilma Martínez*. Austin, TX: Steck-Vaughn Company. Grades 3-5.

Vilma Martínez, a lawyer who challenged many of the laws that discriminated against her fellow Mexican Americans, grew up in San Antonio, Texas, during the time of unfair treatment of Mexican Americans. She helped form the Mexican American Legal Defense and Educational Fund (MALDEF), a group that helps protect the rights of Mexican Americans. Later, she became its chief lawyer and fought against the unfair treatment of Mexican Americans in schools, in the workplace, and in politics. This book, with its muted color illustrations by Susi Kilgore, also provides Spanish text translated by Alma Flor Ada. (Steck-Vaughn's Raintree Hispanic Stories series highlights the contributions of Latinos to the development of the United States. Several titles are mentioned in this chapter.)

Cruz, Manuel, and Cruz, Ruth. (1980). *A Chicano Christmas Story*. South Pasadena, CA: Bilingual Educational Services. Grades 3-5.

This story centers around a Mexican American (or *Chicano*) migrant family and their difficulties during the winter, when there is no work. The fact that Santa Claus is responsible for bringing gifts to children rather than the three wise men, as is the custom of many Latin American countries, is one of the central points of this story.

De Paola, Tomie. (1980). *The Lady of Guadalupe*. New York: Holiday House. Grades 3-5.

The legend of Juan Diego and his vision of Mary, the mother of Jesus, has been part of Mexican tradition for nearly 500 years. It is said that during the month of December in 1531, Juan appeared before the Catholic clergy with roses given to him by Mary. Mexican and Mexican American Catholics continue to celebrate Juan Diego's vision on December 12th, a major Mexican Catholic holiday. The Spanish version of this book has been translated by Pura Belpre. Color illustrations are by the well-known author/illustrator.

FIGURE 3-3 *The Adventures of Connie and Diego* by María García, copyright © 1987 by Children's Book Press. Reprinted by permission of Bookstop Literacy Agency, agent for Children's Book Press.

García, María. (1987). *The Adventures of Connie and Diego. Las aventuras de Connie y Diego.* San Francisco: Children's Book Press. Grades K-2.

Connie and Diego were born different from their brothers and sisters in that they had many colors all over their bodies. They leave their home in "the land of plenty" to avoid the ridicule that comes from being different. With the help of a tiger, they come to realize that, regardless of their color, they are still humans. The need to accept oneself as a part of humanity is a message that should be communicated in every classroom. The colorful illustrations by Malaquias Montoya and the hand-lettered bilingual text make this simple and thought-provoking story a great book for all children of color.

FIGURE 3-4 *Family Pictures/Cuadros de familia* by Carmen Lomas Garza, copyright © 1990 by Carmen Lomas Garza. Reprinted by permission of Bookstop Literacy Agency, agent for Children's Book Press.

Garza, Carmen Lomas. (1990). *Family Pictures. Cuadros de familia.* San Francisco: Children's Book Press. Grades 3-5.

A prominent and upcoming Mexican American artist, Garza shares with the reader experiences from her childhood in South Texas. Children will see pictures of and read about (in both English and Spanish) such experiences as breaking a *piñata*, going to the beach, making *tamales*, and several other cultural activities. Fourteen different activities, some involving the extended family, and 14 paintings are this book's major strengths.

Gleiter, Jan, & Thompson, Kathleen. (1991). *Miguel Hidalgo Y Costilla.* Austin, TX: Steck-Vaughn Company. Grades 3-5.

Miguel Hidalgo y Costilla was a Catholic priest who wanted to help the people of Mexico free themselves from Spain's control. Hidalgo was the first leader in Spanish America who protested black slavery, and he also issued decrees guaranteeing Mexican Indians equal status. Unfortunately, Hidalgo was captured, tried, and shot by the Spanish army before Mexico won its independence from Spain. Although the war for independence lasted another 10 years, Miguel Hidlago is known as the father of Mexican Independence for his courage and commitment to free Mexico. Color illustrations are by Rick Karpiniski. *Miguel Hidalgo y Costilla* is one of four books in Steck-Vaughn's Raintree Hispanic Stories series highlighting the contributions of Mexicans to the Americas. The other books include Jan Gleiter's *Benito Juárez* (1991), Jan Gleiter and Kathleen Thompson's *Diego Rivera* (1991), and Kathleen Thompson's *Sor Juana Inés De La Cruz* (1991).

Hayes, Joe. (1987). *La Llorona: The Weeping Woman.* El Paso, TX: Cinco Puntos Press. Grades 3-5.

María is a beautiful young woman who in a moment of anger throws her children in the river. After realizing what she has done, she spends the night looking for her children. She is found the next morning dead. Now María, the Weeping Woman, is said to be searching the river for her children. Considered by many to be *the* classic folktale of the

FIGURE 3-5 *La Llorona: The Weeping Woman* by Joe Hayes, copyright © Vicki Trejo Hill. Permission granted by Ms. Hill and Cinco Puntos Press, 2709 Louisville, El Paso, TX 79930.

Spanish-speaking people of North America, the legend of *La llorona* has many versions, depending on geographic location and time period. The version presented in this book is from northern New Mexico. The black and white pictures by Vicki Trejo Hill add to the mood of the story.

Hayes, Joe. (1983). *The Day It Snowed Tortillas: Tales From Spanish New Mexico*. Santa Fe, NM: Mariposa Publishing. Grades 3-5.

Seven humorous and entertaining stories filled with Mexican and Mexican American folklore are told in this collection, including the most famous story from Mexico and the Southwest *"La Llorona."* This story of a haunting woman looking for the children she has killed is well known to Mexican and Mexican American children. Hayes has written the tales in the storytelling tradition, making them great for reading aloud.

Munson, Sammye. (1989). *Our Tejano Heroes: Outstanding Mexican-Americans in Texas*. Austin, TX: Eakin Press. Grades 6-8.

Thirty-three significant Mexican Americans are profiled in this easy-to-read book. The lives of contemporary Texans of Mexican descent, or *Tejanos*, such as Lee Treviño, professional golfer, and Henry B. González, U. S. congressman, are told in this book. Also, historical information is provided on *Tejanos* such as José Antonio Navarro, one of the writers of the Texas Constitution.

Palacios, Argentina. (1993). *¡Viva México!: The Story of Benito Juárez and Cinco de Mayo*. Austin, TX: Steck-Vaughn Company.

A Zapotec Indian who began life in a two-room adobe house with a dirt floor, Benito Juárez became one of the best-known presidents of Mexico. Although few opportunities were available for Juárez and other Zapotec Indians to get a formal education, through hard work and determination Juárez became a lawyer who helped his people. Palacios has written a simple story that will appeal to Mexican American children. Benito Juárez exemplifies the spirit of determination against all odds. This book also provides information on the significance of *Cinco de Mayo*, a major holiday for Mexican and Mexican Americans. The color illustrations are by Howard Berelson.

Roberts, Maurice (1991). *Henry Cisneros: A Leader for the Future*. Chicago: Children's Press. Grades 3-5.

Although Cisneros continues to make history (as a member of President Bill Clinton's cabinet), this book centers on his days as mayor of San Antonio, Texas. As the first Latino to be elected mayor of an important U.S. city, Cisneros proved to be a hard worker for San Antonio and all its people. This book, with its black-and-white photographs, provides young Latinos a glimpse into the life of one of the best-known Mexican Americans of our times.

Roberts, Maurice. (1987). *César Chávez and La Causa*. Chicago: Children's Press. Grades 3-5.

In 1962, César Chávez founded the National Farm Workers Association (later renamed the United Farm Workers) to help farm workers improve their working conditions and their wages. Through public support of a boycott of grapes and lettuce, Chávez and his supporters were able to improve the lives of farm workers. Black and white photographs help tell the story of the father of *la Causa* (the cause), the name given to the organization's efforts. Black and white photographs of César Chávez, his followers, and dignitaries that lent their support to *la Causa* are included.

Another book that chronicles the history of the organization of migrant farm workers is Dana de Ruiz's *La Causa: The Farmworkers' Story* (1993). This book from the Steck-Vaughn Company provides a more detailed look at the struggles of the United Farm Workers and César Chávez. From the Stories of America series, this title is recommended for Grades 6–8.

Rohmer, Harriet. (1982). *The Legend of Food Mountain. La montaña del alimento*. San Francisco: Children's Book Press. Grades 3-5.

According to an Aztec legend, *Quetzalcoatl* (pronounced Ket-ZAL-kwatl) was the creator of the first people on Earth. Not knowing what to feed them, he joins a giant red ant on a trip to Food Mountain to search for corn. Quetzalcoatl decides to bring Food Mountain to the people, but unforeseen problems cause his plan to fail. In this bilingual book, Graciela Carrillo's illustrations include symbols from the picture-writing manuscripts of the native Aztec priests. This creation myth shows the value of the preservation of Earth.

Rohmer, Harriet, & Gómez, Cruz. (1989). *Mr. Sugar Came to Town. La visita del Sr. Azúcar*. San Francisco: Children's Book Press. Grades K-2.

This was originally a puppet show, performed for the children in migrant labor camps in California. Mr. Sugar has come to town to seduce Alicia and Alfredo with sweets. They stuff themselves with sweets every day, until one day Grandma Lupe spoils Mr. Sugar's fiendish plan. The English/Spanish text and color illustrations provide an entertaining as well as educational story.

FIGURE 3-6 *Mr. Sugar Comes to Town/La visita del Sr. Azúcar*
by Harriet Rohmer and Cruz Gómez, copyright © 1989 by Children's
Book Press. Reprinted by permission of Bookstop Literacy Agency,
agent for Children's Book Press.

Soto, Gary. (1990). *A Fire in My Hands: A Book of Poems.* New York:
Scholastic. Grades 6-8.

Gary Soto, a Mexican American writer from California, has finally
reached mainstream America with his poems depicting the Mexican
American experience. This collection of 23 poems includes several that
were written in the late 1970s and early 1980s. Soto provides a short
narrative to introduce each poem. This book would be a good addition
to any poetry unit in a language arts curriculum.

Soto, Gary. (1991). *Taking Sides.* New York: Harcourt Brace
Jovanovich. Grades 6-8.

Lincoln Mendoza, an eighth grader, has recently moved from the inner
city to a suburban town. Life is very different in the suburbs, and it will
take time for him to adjust. Playing against friends from his old school
is one of his Lincoln's biggest worries. Soto uses Spanish words,
phrases, and glimpses of Mexican American culture to develop believable Mexican American characters.

Stanek, Muriel. (1989). *I Speak English For My Mom.* Niles, IL: Albert Whitman & Company. Grades 3-5.

This story centers around a young girl, Lupe, who has to help her non-English-speaking mother. Many Hispanic children, not just Mexican Americans, will relate to Lupe's experiences and understand her feelings as she acts as an interpreter for her mother. Although the black and white pictures are not inviting to most children, this story about the immigrant experience needs to be told.

Winter, Jeanette. (1991). *Diego.* New York: Alfred A. Knopf. Grades K-2.

As a child, Diego Rivera loved to draw. Children will enjoy the simplicity of this account of the early years of one of the world's greatest muralists. The beautiful illustrations by Jeanette Winter resemble miniature portraits. Mexican American children will enjoy the last two lines of this English/Spanish book. "His paintings made people proud to be Mexican. They still do."

PUERTO RICAN CHILDREN'S LITERATURE

Unlike undocumented Mexicans living and working in the United States, Puerto Ricans are citizens of the United States and are free to migrate to and from the island of Puerto Rico. According to the 1990 U.S. Census, 2.7 million Puerto Ricans (1.1 percent of the total population) reside in the United States. A comparison between the 1990 and 1980 figures show that the Puerto Rican population in the United States increased by only 700,000 (0.2 percent) in the last 10 years. Most Puerto Ricans live in New York or other northeastern urban areas (Rudman, 1984). The educational status of the predominantly urban Puerto Rican community is disturbing.

Earlier, we mentioned González's (1992) reference to a report from the National Council of La Raza that stated that nearly 50 percent of Mexican Americans drop out before graduating from high school. Unfortunately, the report also states that the same dropout rate applies to Puerto Rican youths. Puerto Rican children must achieve academic success in our educational system if we are to begin to address the problems that keep 41 percent of the Puerto Rican population in poverty (Tharp, Whitman, & Streisand, 1992). Puerto Rican children, like Mexican Americans and other Latinos, must be given an opportunity to learn through literature that speaks to them—stories that are filled with their culture and that celebrate its uniqueness. Currently, few books are available that depict with accuracy the quality of the Puerto Rican experience (de Cortes, 1992). Listed below are resources that provide positive images of Puerto Ricans and that are valuable in helping children appreciate Puerto Rican culture.

Chrisman, Abbott. (1991). *Luis Muñoz Marín*. Austin, TX: Steck-Vaughn Company. Grades 3-5.

The son of Premier Luís Muñoz Rivera, the first native-born leader of Puerto Rico, Luís Muñoz Marín also was destined to make history in his native Puerto Rico. The people of Puerto Rico were living under terrible conditions. There were inadequate jobs, schools, hospitals, and housing. Muñoz Marín helped bring about many changes that benefitted the *jíbaros* (the impoverished people of Puerto Rico). This book, from the Raintree Hispanic Stories series, provides an interesting and informative look at one of the best-known Puerto Ricans. The well-written Spanish text is translated by Gloria Contreras.

FIGURE 3-7 *My Aunt Otilia's Spirits/Los espíritus de mi Tía Otilia* by Richard García, copyright © 1987 by Children's Book Press. Reprinted by permission of Bookstop Literacy Agency, agent for Children's Book Press.

Coll y Toste, Cayetano. (1988). *Puerto Rican Tales: Legends of Colonial Spanish times.* Mayagüez, Puerto Rico: Ediciones Librero. Grades 3-5.

These 12 legends, dating from 1511 to 1840, provide a glimpse into Puerto Rico's culture and history. The lives of the Taino Indians (the Native people of Puerto Rico), the Spanish Conquistadores, and the African slaves are vividly described in these legends. The stories, translated and adapted in English by Dr. José Ramírez Rivera, tell of adventure, romance, history, and religion.This book is an important resource for the English-speaking Puerto Rican child living in the United States.

Crespo, George. (1993). *How the Sea Began.* New York: Clarion Books. Grades K-2.

A Taino creation myth, this is the story of how the islands inhabited by the Taino Indians in the Caribbean Sea were created. Illustrated by the author, this story reflects the Taino culture that, along with the Spanish and African cultures, has influenced today's Puerto Rican culture. This is the author's first book.

García, Richard. (1987). *My Aunt Otilia's Spirits. Los espíritus de mi Tía Otilia.* San Francisco: Children's Book Press. Grades K-2.

When Aunt Otilia comes to visit her nephew in the United States, peculiar things begin to happen. Aunt Otilia tries to calm her nephew by telling him it is only her noisy spirits, but when Aunt Otilia's bones leave her body one night, the excitement is a just a little too much for the young boy! This colorful book, illustrated by Robin Cherin and Roger Reyes, is written in both English and Spanish. Children will enjoy this scary yet funny story.

Hurwitz, Johanna. (1990). *Class President.* New York: Morrow Junior Books. Grades 3-5.

Julio Sánchez, first introduced to readers in Hurwitz's *Class Clown* (1987) and *Teacher's Pet* (1988), is the fifth-grade campaign manager for Lucas Cott who is running for class president. The race between his friend the class clown and Cricket Kaufman, last year's teacher's pet, is close, but it is Julio who might be the best candidate. With the help of his fifth grade teacher, Ernesto Flores, Julio becomes aware of his Puerto Rican heritage. Although the story is lacking in references to Puerto Rican culture, Hurwitz's depiction of Ernesto Flores (as a strong Latino role model) makes this story exemplary.

Mohr, Nicholasa. (1989). *Felita.* New York: Bantam Doubleday Dell Publishing. Grades 6-8.

Felita, an eight-year-old girl, and her family move from their *barrio* or Puerto Rican neighborhood, to a new neighborhood where she experiences discrimination. Felita's father moved his family so that his children would have a better education, but Felita and her three brothers soon realize that they are not welcome in their new neighborhood. The entire family finally comes to the realization that they must leave before they are seriously hurt. Throughout the ordeal, Felita is comforted by her grandmother. The wisdom and love shown by her grandmother leave a lasting impression on Felita even after her grandmother dies. This is an excellent book that shows the strong bonds in many of our Latino extended families.

Mohr, Nicholasa. (1986). *Going Home.* New York: Dutton/Dial. Grades 6-8.

In this book, Mohr's sequel to *Felita*, the twelve-year-old, Felita and her family are going to spend a two-week summer vacation in Puerto Rico. Thanks to Tío Jorge, her uncle, Felita will have the opportunity to stay in Puerto Rico for the entire summer. Felita's excitement at this prospect of freedom is quickly dashed when she is sent to stay with a strict aunt and uncle. She also begins to feel a strain in her relationship with her cousins because she and her brothers are *Nuyoricans* (Puerto Ricans born and/or raised in the United States). This book is effective in showing how cultural differences may cause problems even within families. Also, children will appreciate Felita's efforts and desire as an adolescent to become more independent.

Mohr Nicholasa. (1993). *All For The Better: A Story of El Barrio.* Austin, TX: Steck-Vaughn Company. Grades 3-5.

Set in the 1930s during the Great Depression, this is a true story based on the life of Evelina López. Evilina's mother decides to send the 11-year-old girl to New York to live with her aunt, Tía Vicenta. In New York, she soon became a very resourceful person in the community. This story by a noted Puerto Rican author provides a vivid account of life in the *barrio* and how a close-knit Puerto Rican community worked together to survive the Great Depression. The story, with its black-and-white illustrations, will help Latino children see the benefits of caring and giving.

Pomerantz, Charlotte. (1980). *The Tamarindo Puppy and Other Poems.* New York: Greenwillow Books. Grades K-2.

Several of the poems in this book mention aspects of Puerto Rican life, such as *pan de agua* (a bread similar to French bread), the towns in "The Four Brothers," and the code-switching between English and Spanish. The intermixing of English and Spanish will appeal to Puerto Rican children who use Spanglish or Mexican Americans who use Tex-Mex in every-day speech. This book will help develop self-esteem among Puerto Rican children.

Rappoport, Ken. (1993). *Bobby Bonilla.* New York: Walker & Company. Grades 3-5.

As the highest paid professional baseball player, Bonilla has risen to stardom in a relatively short period of time. After spending six years with the Pittsburgh Pirates, Bonilla signed a contract with the New York Mets for nearly $30 million. The story and photographs of this young Puerto Rican born in New York City on February 23, 1963, will entertain young baseball fans.

Rohmer, Harriet. & Rea, Jesús G. (1988). *Atariba & Niguayona: A Story from the People of Puerto Rico.* San Francisco: Children's Book Press. Grades K-2.

In English and Spanish, Rohmer and Rea tell the story of Niguayona, a hero of the Tainos, the native people of Puerto Rico. When his friend Atariba becomes ill, Niguayona leaves his village and with the help of plants and animals begins to search for the healing *caimini* tree. Children will enjoy the story of a small child fearlessly searching for the magical fruit that will help save his little friend. He accomplishes his goal through is oneness with nature rather than through an attempt to harness it. The authors

FIGURE 3-8 *Three Kings' Day* by Beatriz McConnie Zapater. © 1992 by The Children's Museum, Boston. Cover reprinted by permission of Modern Curriculum Press.

provide information on the Taino people and their culture at the end of the book. Colorful illustrations by Consuelo Méndez and pronunciations of the Taino words make this story informative and entertaining.

Zapater, Beatriz M. (1992). *Three Kings' Day*. Cleveland, OH: Modern Curriculum Press. Grades 3-5.

Melinda and Fernando, two young Puerto Rican children living in the United States, prepare for the celebration of Three Kings' Day on January 6. While most North American children receive their gifts from Santa Claus on Christmas morning, Puerto Rican children wait for their gifts from the Three Wise Kings (the Three Wise Men). This book, from the Multicultural Celebration series, provides a glimpse into one family's traditions and rituals on the eve of Three Kings' Day. The pastel illustrations by Nayda Collazo Llorens offer images of Puerto Rican culture, such as the preparation of foods and the holiday music. A glossary of Spanish words associated with this celebration is provided at the end.

LITERATURE FOR AND ABOUT OTHER LATINOS

The following list includes books about specific Latino communities other than the Mexican American and Puerto Rican. The cultural group depicted in each book is indicated in parentheses. Note that books that do not specify a particular culture but do concern a character or characters who are Latino have also been included in this section. These books will indicate Latino in parenthesis. Books that are collections of stories, poems, or biographies about various Latinos are also included in this section and will also indicate Latino.

Christopher, Matt. (1992). *Centerfield Ballhawk*. Boston: Little, Brown and Company. Grades 6-8. (Latino)

Christopher, who has written over 30 sports novels, introduces readers to José Méndez (the accent mark is omitted from "Méndez" in the text of this book). José, a nine-year-old, is one of the best outfielders for the Peach Tree Mudders. Since his father, Mr. Méndez, was once a minor-league slugger, José would rather be known for his hitting than for his fielding. Mr. Méndez is a good role model for children. However, neither the text nor the illustrations help us determine whether José is Mexican American, Cuban American, or of any specific Latino group. Although Latino culture is not an integral part of the story, Christopher has nonetheless provided Latino children with a protagonist they will be able to relate to. Christopher's expertise in describing play-by-play action is the true strength of this story.

Codye, Corinn. (1991). *Luis W. Alvarez*. Austin, TX: Steck-Vaughn Company. Grades 3-5. (Latino)

Alvarez, a 1968 Nobel Prize winner in physics, was one of the nuclear scientists who worked on the atomic bomb during World War II. The bilingual text, written by Alma Flor Ada, provides an informative look at one of the leading Latinos in science. Two other notable books from the Raintree Hispanic Stories series are Abbott Chrisman's *David Farragut* (1991), the story of a Spanish American Union admiral born in Tennessee, and Jan Gleiter and Kathleen Thompson's *José Martí* (1991), about the Cuban author who fought for Cuba's independence from Spain.

Delacre, Lulu. (1989). *Arroz Con Leche: Popular Songs and Rhymes From Latin America.* New York: Scholastic. Grades K-2. (Latino).

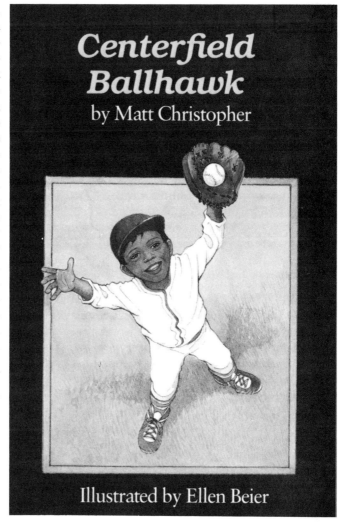

FIGURE 3-9 *Centerfield Ballhawk* by Matt Christopher. Copyright © 1992 by Little, Brown and Company. Reprinted by permission of Little, Brown and Company.

Three of the songs in this book originate from Mexico, the others are from Puerto Rico and Argentina. These Spanish songs and their English translations permeate Latino culture. This book will be very entertaining to Latino as well as to non-Latino children because of its rhythmic verses.

de Varona, Frank. (1991). *Bernardo de Gálvez.* Austin, TX: Steck-Vaughn Company. Grades 3-5. (Spanish)

At the age of 16, Bernardo de Gálvez joined the Spanish Army. At the age of 29, having been appointed governor of the Louisiana Territory, he helped the Americans during the Revolutionary War. Before he died at the age of 40, de Gálvez had accomplished many things and was considered a compassionate person who tried to help the people he governed.

This is one of 16 books (all with English/Spanish text) in Steck-Vaughn's Raintree Hispanic Stories series that highlight Latino contributions to America. Other stories from the series that recount the exploits of people from Spain who left their mark in the Americas are Abbott Chrisman's *Hernando de Soto* (1991), Corinn Codye's *Queen Isabella I* (1991), Jan Gleiter and Kathleen Thompson's *Pedro Menéndez de Avilés* (1991), and Kathleen Thompson's *Junípero Serra* (1991).

Hewett, Joan. (1990). *Laura Loves Horses.* New York: Clarion Books. Grades 3-5. (Latino)

Laura Santana, age eight, spends her days caring for and riding horses on the farm where her father works. This photo essay, with pictures by Richard Hewett, would have to be considered a melting-pot book, since no specific Latino culture is identified. The book does, however, provide Latino children with an opportunity to see a young Latina working and having fun with horses.

McLerran, Alice. (1992). *I Want To Go Home.* New York: Tambourine Books. Grades 3-5. (Latino)

Marta, a young Latina, does not like the new house she and Mama have moved into. In an effort to please Marta, Mama has brought a cat home, but he's not happy either! Marta seems to be an assimilated middle-class Latino child, and the book lacks information that would give Marta a stronger Latino heritage. All in all, the story shows a young girl struggling with the problem of coping with change. The underlying theme is adjusting to change, and this melting-pot book allows children to express their feelings and views about Marta's feelings and experiences as well as their own.

Peña, Sylvia C. (ed.). (1990). *Kikirikí: Stories and Poems in English and Spanish for Children.* Houston, TX: Arte Público Press. Grades K-2, 3-5. (Latino)

The works of Mexican American, Puerto Rican, Cuban American, and other Latino poets and writers reflecting their individual cultures are the focal point of this book. Thirteen-Spanish language poems and short stories and 15 English-language poems and short stories concern various aspects of growing up Latino in the United States. The works of two notable writers, Sandra Cisneros (Mexican American) and Nicholassa Mohr (Puerto Rican), are included.

Peña, Sylvia C. (ed.). (1986). *TUN-TA-CA-TUN: More Stories and Poems in English and Spanish for Children.* Houston, TX: Arte Público Press. Grades 3-5. (Latino)

This collection of poems and short stories from Mexican American and Puerto Rican writers is a sequel to *Kikirikí*. Along with stories and poems about the Latino experience in the United States is a story about an indigenous group from Mexico, "Sunkissed: An Indian Leg-

TUN-TA-CA-TUN

More Stories and Poems in English and Spanish for Children

Edited by Sylvia Cavazos Peña

FIGURE 3-10 *Tun-Ta-Ca-Tun: More Stories and Poems in English and Spanish for Children* (1986) by Sylvia Cavazos Peña. Cover reprinted by permission of Arte Público Press.

end." Nicholassa Mohr's "Jaime and the Conch Shell," the story of a lonesome five-year-old Puerto Rican boy struggling to adjust to his new surroundings in the United States, is an excellent story about the immigrant experience.

Perl, Lila. (1983). *Piñatas and Paper Flowers: Holidays of the Americas in English and Spanish. Piñatas y flores de papel: Fiestas de las Américas en inglés y español.* New York: Clarion Books. Grades 6-8. (Latino)

Eight holidays celebrated by Latinos in different parts of North, Central, and South America are featured in this bilingual book, which describes specific traditions from various countries in the celebration of the same holiday. Although there are similarities in how New Year's Eve is celebrated, for example, there are also differences. In Mexico, firecrackers are put on a wooden frame resembling a castle and then lit. In Puerto Rico, a bucket of water is splashed across your path (or on you!) at the stroke of midnight. In Ecuador, a scarecrow, symbolic of the old year is burned. This is very informative book that will be a great resource for the classroom.

Powers, Thomas J. & Galvan, José L. (1989). *Champions of Change: Biographies of Famous Hispanic Americans.* Austin, TX: Steck-Vaughn Company. Grades 3-5. (Latino)

Ten Latinos are featured in this workbook-type collection of biographies. Among the better known Latinos are Roberto Clemente, the Puerto Rican baseball player; José Feliciano, the Puerto Rican musician; and Jim Plunkett, the Mexican American professional football player. Also featured are Franklin Chang-Diaz, one of the first Latino astronauts, and Tracie Ruiz, a two-time Olympic gold medalist. At the end of each biography a set of questions is provided to aid in comprehension. Although unattractive in its layout, this book with its black and white photographs does provide factual and interesting information.

Rohmer, Harriet. (1989). *Uncle Nacho's Hat. El sombrero del Tío Nacho.* San Francisco: Children's Book Press. Grades 3-5. (Nicaraguan)

Rohmer's book, with Spanish translation by Alma Flor Ada, is a Nicaraguan folktale about a man who cannot get rid of an old hat. His niece, Ambrosia, having heard Uncle Nacho complain every morning about his old hat, gives him a new one. With the help of Ambrosia, he is able to begin to enjoy the new hat. Children will enjoy reading this comical story and looking at the colorful pictures by Veg Reisberg. Exposure to folk tales of Hispanic origins is an important element in developing the self-identity of Latino children.

Rohmer, Harriet, Chow, Octavio, & Vidaure, Morris. (1987). *The Invisible Hunters. Los cazadores invisibles.* San Francisco: Children's Book Press. Grades 3-5. (Nicaraguan)

With collage-style color illustrations, this magical tale from the indigenous people of Nicaragua tells of the danger of forgetting the traditional ways. The lesson of the story, that greed eventually destroys a person, is common to every culture. From the Stories from Central America series, this well-written story lends itself to reading aloud. Contains both English and Spanish text.

Sinnott, Susan. (1991). *Extraordinary Hispanic Americans.* Chicago: Children's Press. Grades 6-8. (Latino)

The people presented in this book have made important contributions to North American culture. The book is divided into five sections: An Age of Exploration, Early Hispanic America, America from Sea to Sea, The Twentieth Century, and Looking Toward the Twenty-First Century. The accomplishments of the people described range from exploring the New World, to contributing to science, medicine, sports, and the arts. This is an excellent resource that provides several short biographies of some lesser known contributors to the American way of life.

FIGURE 3-11 *Fiesta!* by Beatriz McConnie Zapater. © 1992 by The Children's Museum, Boston. Cover reprinted by permission of Modern Curriculum Press.

Smith, Marylou M. (1984). *Grandmother's Adobe House.* Santa Fe, NM: New Mexico Magazine. Grades 3-5. (Latino)

Mexicans, Pueblo Indians, Navajo Indians, Spanish, and Anglos have all had an impact on the New Mexican adobe house. This book, with color illustrations by Ann Blackstone, provides an informative look at the adobe house and its furnishings. Throughout the English text, a pronunciation key is provided to explain how to say each Spanish word.

Van Loan, Nancy. (1991). *El Dorado*. New York: Alfred A. Knopf. Grades 3-5. (South American)

A folktale first told in Colombia, *El Dorado*, is the story of a queen and her daughter who leave the king one night to live in the palace of an emerald serpent in Lake Guatavita. The king, longing for his family, is comforted by the serpent, who promises him that someday he will be allowed to join his family. This is an entertaining story with well-written text and beautifully colored illustrations by Beatriz Vidal.

Zapater, Beatriz McConnie. (1992). *Fiesta!* Cleveland, OH: Modern Curriculum Press. Grades 3-5. (Colombian)

Chucho, a young Colombian American boy, prepares for a fiesta like the ones in Colombia. His parents, Mami and Papi, provide him with information about the history and traditions of the fiesta. From Modern Curriculum's Multicultural Celebrations series, this book was illustrated by José Ortega and created under the auspices of The Children's Museum in Boston. The strength of the series is that each book is written in consultation with someone from the culture described. Other titles in the series may be found in other chapters of this book.

REFERENCES

De Cortes, O. G. (1992). United States: Hispanic Americans. In Miller-Lachmann, L. (ed.). *Our Family, our friends, our world: Annotated guide to significant multicultural books for children and teenagers.* New Providence, NJ: R. R. Bowker.

González, R. D. (1992). When minority becomes majority: The changing face of English classrooms. *English Journal, 79,* 16-23.

Etts, H. (1967). *Bad Boy, Good Boy.* New York: Crowell.

Tharp, M., Whitman, D., & Streisand, B. (1992, May 25). Hispanics' tale of two cities. *U.S. New & World Report,* pp. 40-41.

Rudman, M. K. (1984). *Children's Literature: An Issues Approach* (2nd ed). New York: Longman.

Schon, I. (1988). Hispanic Books. Libros Hispanos. *Young Children, 23,* 81-85.

AFRICAN AMERICAN CHILDREN'S LITERATURE

African Americans have in general fared better than other ethnic groups in their depiction in children's books. Although the supply of books published for and about African Americans continues to be small, more books for African American children are available than for other children of color (Swanson, 1992). Many contemporary books depict African Americans' experiences in terms that are universal in that many children, regardless of race or ethnicity, can identify with them. Other stories provide the reader with a more in-depth look at African American traditions, values, and beliefs.

The books in this chapter are divided into three categories: Contemporary Settings, African American Traditions, and People to Remember. Books listed under the first category explore such aspects of contemporary life within African American culture as the extended family (Hoffman, Payne, & Smith, 1992). Some of these books concern grandparents, aunts, or uncles who provide African American children with stories of a proud history or offer support in a time of trouble.

Storytelling is an important aspect of the African American experience. The section entitled African American Traditions focuses on books that provide information about and insight into storytelling and other cultural traditions of the African American community. Titles listed under the third category are biographies or historical fiction highlighting the contributions of African Americans to American society and to people throughout the world. For example, Matthew Henson, who until recently was omitted from history books, was the co-discoverer of the North Pole with Robert Peary. The following books provide the reader with an opportunity to experience vicariously some of the heart and soul of the African American experience.

CONTEMPORARY SETTINGS

Blackman, Marjorie. (1992). *A New Dress for Maya.* Milwaukee: Gareth Stevens Children's Books. Grades K–2.

Originally published in Great Britain in 1991, this story centers around a young girl who would like to buy a particular dress to wear to a friend's birthday party. Maya pouts, shouts, and cries when told by several relatives that she cannot have the dress from the store, because her mother is making her a dress. At the party she finds out why it was best for her to wear the dress her mother made her. The water color drawings by Rhian Nest James are exceptional depictions of a loving extended family.

Brown, Kay. (1990). *Willy's Summer Dream.* New York: Harcourt Brace Jovanovich. Grades 6–8.

Willie is a 14-year-old boy living in a single-parent home who has a learning disability. His summer vacation is quite boring until his neighbor's niece comes for a visit. Willy is enamored of the beautiful Katherine, but she is older than he and tends to treat him more as a mother. By the time she leaves, her tutoring of Willy in reading has improved his self-esteem. Profanity is used in this book, but it gives the story its realistic flavor. Set in Brooklyn, the story provides the reader with glimpses of African American culture.

Caines, Jeannette. (1982). *Just Us Women.* New York: Harper & Row. Grades K–2.

This is an excellent story about a young African American girl and her aunt traveling in a new car. The pictures by Pat Cummings and the words of the author show a young girl experiencing life not at the poverty level, but rather enjoying a meal at a fancy restaurant and taking a leisurely trip across several states.

Cameron, Ann. (1990). *Julian, Dream Doctor.* New York: Random House. Grades 3–5.

Julian, a young African American boy, decides that the gift he gets for his Dad this year will be special—something his Dad has always dreamed of. The only problem is that Julian does not know what that special something is! Considered a melting-pot book, this is nevertheless a very entertaining story that will have children laughing at Julian trying to identify and locate a special gift for his Dad. Other stories by Cameron featuring Julian are *The Stories Julian Tells* (1981), *More Stories Julian Tells* (1986), *Julian's Glorious Summer* (1987), and *Julian, Secret Agent* (1988).

Clifton, Lucille. (1983). *Everett Anderson's Goodbye.* New York: Henry Holt Company. Grades K–2.

Clifton has written several books with strong African American characters. This story centers around Everett's feelings after his father dies.

The five stages of Everett's grief are denial, anger, bargaining, depression, and acceptance. The story is simply told in a poetic style and is illustrated by Ann Grifalconi.

Clifton's *Amifika* (1977), the story of a young boy who, along with his mother, awaits his father's return from the army, is another good book for the grades K–2 group. When Amifika's mother begins to throw things out of the house to make room for his Dad, Amifika begins to worry that she may throw him out!

Crews, Donald. (1991). *Bigmama's.* New York: Greenwillow Books. Grades K–2.

Crews reflects, through words and pictures, on his summer trips to the country to visit his grandmother—Bigmama. Nothing ever changes at Bigmama's. Even the conductor tells the same joke every year as the train nears Cottondale, Florida. The love and happiness that Crews's fond recollections of his childhood communicate will have children coming back to the book again and again.

Fields, Julia. (1988). *The Green Lion of Zion Street.* New York: McElderry. Grades 3–5.

This is a narrative poem set in the inner city. A group of African American children walk into a foggy park where a green statue of a lion sits on a pedestal. What happens next will captivate the reader! This book captures the storytelling tradition of African Americans.

Havill, Juanita. (1989). *Jamaica Tag-along.* Boston: Houghton Mifflin Company. Grades K–2.

When Jamaica's older brother goes to the park to play basketball, she tags along, hoping she will be allowed to play. Unable to convince her brother and his three friends to let her play, she goes to the sandbox and meets a little boy named Berto. Jamaica comes to relate to her older brother's feelings when Berto becomes a tag along. The watercolors by Anne Sibley O'Brien capture the spirit of Jamaica and the other characters.

Howard, Elizabeth F. (1991). *Aunt Flossie's Hats (and Crab Cakes Later).* New York: Clarion Books. Grades 3–5.

Howard's book, beautifully illustrated by James Ransome, tells the story of two sisters' visit to their great-great-aunt Flossie. The house is full of interesting things, but the hats are what the girls enjoy the most because Aunt Flossie has a story to tell with each hat. The loving relationships that exist in this extended family are revealed through well-written text and realistic oil paintings in deep, rich colors.

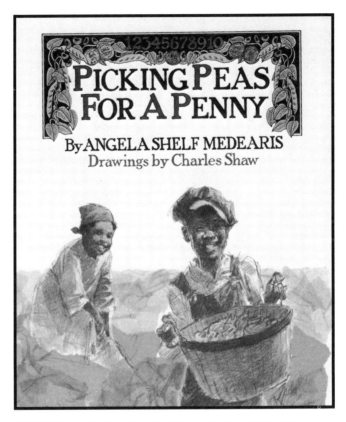

FIGURE 4-1 *Picking Peas for A Penny* by Angela Shelf Medearis (1990). Cover reprinted by permission of State House Press.

Medearis, Angela S. (1990). *Picking Peas for a Penny.* Austin, TX: State House Press. Grades K–2.

Set in the depression of the 1930s, Medearis's simple and charming book tells of the hard work and joys of life on the farm. Even though picking peas is hard work, the young girl who tells the story still has fun working under the hot sun. Also, there are nice things to buy with the money she earns to make it all seem worthwhile. The poetic language will appeal to children; the black and white pencil drawings are by Charles Shaw.

Smothers, Ethel Footman. (1992). *Down in the Piney Woods.* New York: Alfred A. Knopf. Grades 6–8.

Set in 1950s rural Georgia, the daily life of 10-year-old Annie Rye is described in a wonderful and enlightening manner. Smothers does an excellent job of character development in this story of a strong African

American family that adjusts to the addition of three half-sisters who come to live with them. Some people have compared this story to Mildred Taylor's *Roll of Thunder Hear My Cry* (1976), although it is not as dramatic. This is Smothers' first novel for children.

Stock, Catherine. (1990). *Halloween Monster*. New York: Bradbury Press. Grades K–2.

Tommy, an African American boy, has decided not to go trick-or-treating this year because it is too scary. However, with the help of his mother, who makes him a Halloween costume, he overcomes his fears and goes out on Halloween night. This story teaches that it is all right to be afraid, and that fears can be overcome.

Tate, Eleanora E. (1990). *Thank You, Dr. Martin Luther King, Jr.* New York: Bantam Doubleday Dell Publishing. Grades 3–5.

Mary Elouise, an African American fourth-grade girl, would like Brandy—blue-eyed, tanned, and blonde—to be her best friend. Mary Elouise does not appreciate her African heritage and would rather not hear about such things as slavery and Dr. King, until two African American storytellers come to her school. The strength of this story is that it encourages a more positive attitude in African Americans as well as other children of color who are ashamed or unappreciative of their cultural differences.

Taylor, Mildred. (1990). *Mississippi Bridge*. New York: Dial. Grades 3–5.

Through the eyes of a white child, Jeremy Simms, Taylor tells this story depicting the life of African Americans and whites in rural Mississippi during the depression. When African American passengers are forced off the bus to make room for several white late-comers, the events that follow bring both the black and white communities together. The Logan family, the main characters in Taylor's *Roll of Thunder, Hear My Cry* (1976), play a small, but significant part. This story is well told and helps the reader get a picture of life and attitudes in during the 1930s. The award-winning author's *Friendship and The Gold Cadillac* (1987) provides a more personal view of some of the injustices endured by African Americans, and of how the strength of the African American family helps them overcome inequality.

Taylor, Mildred. (1990). *The Road To Memphis*. New York: Dutton. Grades 6–8.

Cassie Logan, first introduced to readers as a fourth-grader growing up in Mississippi in *Roll of Thunder, Hear My Cry* (1976), is now a 17-year-old high school senior in 1941. Cassie has a close-knit family whose love for each other helps them endure the injustices and other hardships of life in America. This is an inspiring story of a young girl's experiences of humiliating racist attacks on African Americans. After Moe, a friend of Cassie's, finally lashes out in self-defense, he flees to Memphis with the help of a young white man. The story chronicles the life of African Americans in pre-World War II America, and gives young people a better understanding of what it means to be an African American today. Taylor's *Let The Circle Be Unbroken* (1981), the second book in the trilogy featuring Cassie Logan, is also an outstanding book on the African American experience.

Walter, Mildred Pitts. (1989). *Have a Happy . . . A Novel.* New York: Lothrop, Lee & Shepard Books. Grades 6–8.

Walter introduces us to a young man, Chris, whose father has been out of work for 18 months. Christmas and Kwanzaa, the seven-day African American celebration, are just around the corner. The fact that Chris's birthday also falls on December 25th doesn't help matters. Chris's warm family, including his Uncle Roland, provides the reader with positive feelings about the African American family.

Another book by Mildred Pitts Walter appropriate for grades 6–8 is *Justin and the Best Biscuits in the World* (1986), also published by Lothrop, Lee and Shepard. This story centers around a 10-year old boy who thinks housework is woman's work until he goes to his grandfather's ranch.

Yarborough, Camille. (1990). *The Shimmershine Queens.* New York: Alfred A. Knopf. Grades 6–8.

Through the stories of a 90-year-old woman, Angie, a fifth-grader, learns of her people's struggles and determination to improve their lives through formal education. Cousin Seatta's stories and lessons instill in Angie a pride in her African heritage. Angie has learned from Seatta that dreaming about better things to come (the get-up gift) and working to achieve that dream (the shimmershine) helped her ancestors survive. For African American children the lesson of this novel is clear: be proud of your heritage and work to achieve your dreams. Yarborough has written a culturally conscious book with a powerful story using African American dialect and an inner-city setting.

AFRICAN AMERICAN TRADITIONS

Storytelling is an important element in the culture of African Americans. Many African American stories have been handed down for centuries, having first been told somewhere on the African continent. However, the writing and publication of African children's literature for and by Africans have been neglected for too long (Osa, 1985). These stories would provide a basis for comparison of African culture and African American culture. Fortunately, some of the stories from Africa have been preserved.

Among the stories from Africa that have survived in America are folktales. African Americans changed these stories to fit their new surroundings and situation as slaves in the New World. For example, slaves told stories of people who escaped to freedom by flying. This African American motif is used in Faith Ringgold's book, *Tar Beach* (1991), a contemporary story of a young girl who envisions ways of helping her family. Similarly, African American slaves used the rabbit to represent the slave condition in many of their stories. The rabbit was defenseless like them, but he was cunning enough to stay alive (Hamilton, 1987). African Americans referred to him as Brother Rabbit (it appears in print in the black vernacular as Bruh Rabbit or Brer Rabbit).

Many of these stories of the people and places of the Old American South are still being told and written down today. Virginia Hamilton's *The People Could Fly: American Black Folktales* (1985), a collection of stories from the days of slavery, contains a story about flying to freedom as well as animal stories.

Another tradition is the celebration of the holiday called *Kwanzaa*, a seven-day celebration of African American culture beginning on December 26th. *Kwanzaa*, created in 1966 by Maulana Karenga, is a time to reflect on the African American experience, past, present, and future, in terms of seven principles: unity, self-determination, collective work, cooperative economics, purpose, creativity, and faith (Kantrowitz and Wiley, 1988). Certain symbols, rituals, foods, and African words have become an important part of this relatively new holiday.

Listed below are books that will help the reader gain a better understanding of African American culture. Included are several African and African American folktales involving animal characters as well as humans who perform extraordinary feats. Books providing information on *Kwanzaa* are also listed.

Aardema, Verna. (1991). *Traveling to Tongo: A Tale of the Nkundo of Zaire.* Grades K–2.

Aardema retells the story of Bowane, a civet cat who is going to marry a civet from another village. After returning home for the bride price, Bowane sets off with three attendants, a pigeon, a python, and a tortoise, to get married. The trip takes several years, and by the time Bowane arrives the bride has married another. The moral of the story is that a person must say no once in a while, even to friends! Lonkundo, the language of the inhabitants of the rain forest of Zaire, is used sparingly throughout the text. A glossary and pronunciation guide are provided. Other noteworthy traditional African tales by Aardema are *Behind the Back of the Mountain* (1973, Dial), *Bringing the Rain to Kapiti Plain: A Nandi Tale* (1981, Dial) and *Why Mosquitoes Buzz in People's Ears* (1975, Dial).

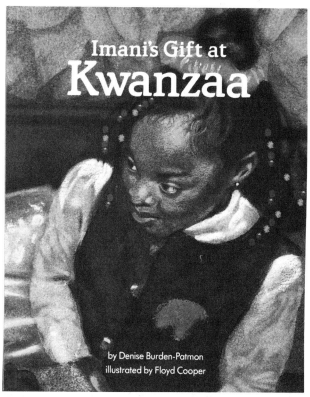

FIGURE 4-2 *Imani's Gift at Kwanzaa* by Burden-Patmon. © 1992 by The Children's Museum, Boston. Cover reprinted by permission of Modern Curriculum Press.

Burden-Patmon, Denise. (1992). *Imani's Gift at Kwanzaa.* Cleveland: Modern Curriculum Press, Inc. Grades 3–5.

Through the eyes of Imani, a young girl, we participate in an evening celebration of *Kwanzaa.* Various rituals, such as the lighting of a candle for every day of the seven-day celebration, are mentioned. This book was developed under the auspices of The Children's Museum of Boston, and is one in a series depicting multicultural celebrations. A glossary of Swahili words used in celebrating the holiday is provided.

FIGURE 4-3 *Kwanzaa* by A.P. Porter. Illustrations by Janice Lee Porter. Copyright 1991 by Carolrhoda Books, Minneapolis.

Chocolate, Deborah M. Newton. (1990). *KWANZAA.* Chicago: Children's Press. Grades 3–5.

The details of the rituals and customs of the celebration of *Kwanzaa* are provided in this story illustrated by Melodye Rosales. The African dress and language used during the holiday are also described. This is an excellent book for instilling pride among African American children in their African ancestry.

Hamilton, Virginia. (1985). *The People Could Fly: American Black Folktales.* New York: Alfred A. Knopf. Grades 6–8.

Hamilton divides this book of African American folktales into animal stories, stories with tall-tale qualities, supernatural tales, and slave tales of freedom. At the conclusion of each story, the author provides the reader with a brief history or variations on the story. Leo and Diane Dillon's illustrations and Hamilton's storytelling make this a truly valuable collection of African American literature.

Knutson, Barbara. (1990). *How the Guinea Fowl Got Her Spots.* Minneapolis: Carolrhoda Books. Grades K–2.

Knutson tells and illustrates a creation story from Swahili of how Nganga (pronounced n'GAHN-gah) the Guinea Fowl, who had glossy black feathers, helped save her friend Cow from Lion. Cow returns the favor by dipping her tail in milk and splattering Nganga with white speckles so that Lion will not recognize her. Knutson's *Why The Crab Has No Head* (1987), a creation story from Zaire also published by Carolrhoda, is appropriate for Grades K–2.

McKissak, Patricia C. (1992). *A Million Fish . . . More or Less.* New York: Alfred A. Knopf. Grades K–2.

This book, with colorful illustrations by Dena Schutzer, tells a story from lower Louisiana called the Bayou Clapateaux. Having caught a million and three fish in a half-hour, Hugh Thomas gets home with only enough fish for dinner. It seems that stories are often stretched a bit in the Bayou, and Hugh Thomas has a story to tell! The beautiful watercolor illustrations are by Dena Schutzer.

McKissak, Patricia C. (1988). *Mirandy and Brother Wind.* New York: Alfred A. Knopf. Grades 3–5.

In her note, McKissak explains that the cakewalk is a dance originating in African American culture. This story is about a young girl named Mirandy who would like to catch the wind (Brother Wind) so that she can win the junior cakewalk with his help. Jerry Pinkney's illustrations complement McKissak's telling of this story of the African American experience at the turn of the century.

McKissak, Patricia C. (1989). *Nettie Jo's Friends.* New York: Alfred A. Knopf. Grades 3–5.

Nettie Jo needs a needle to sew a new dress for her favorite doll so that they can both go to a wedding. As she searches for a needle she helps Miz Rabbit, Fox, and Panther, but they have no time to help her. This story reminiscent of the Old South will delight children as they share Nettie Jo's dilemma. Scott Cook's oil paintings help develop the different personalities of the characters. Another delightful tale from the rural South by McKissack is *Flossie & the Fox* (1986, Dial), with beautiful illustrations by noted author Rachel Isadora that capture the story's funny moments.

Porter, A.A. (1991). *KWANZAA*. Minneapolis: Carolrhoda Books. Grades 3–5.

The purpose, history, and customs of the relatively young African American holiday *Kwanzaa* are clearly explained in this book. The last page provides a basic list of items needed to celebrate *Kwanzaa*. A glossary of Swahili words used in the celebration is provided at the beginning and end of the book. The color illustrations by Janice Lee Porter provide vivid pictures of the celebration.

Price, Loentyne. (1990). *Aïda*. New York: Harcourt Brace Jovanovich. Grades 3–5.

Based on the opera by Guiseppe Verdi, this moving love story will appeal to young and old alike. Aïda is an Ethiopian princess who is captured and enslaved by the Egyptians, who are at war with Ethiopia. She is made a handmaiden to the princess of Egypt, who is in love with the leader of the Egyptian army. Aïda finds herself in a dilemma when she falls in love with the same Egyptian warrior. Aïda must somehow choose between the man she loves and her family and country. The illustrations by the award-winning couple Leo and Diane Dillon are exceptional, vividly complementing the story.

Rosales, Melodye. (1991). *Double Dutch and the Voodoo Shoes*. Chicago: Children's Press. Grades K–2.

This book, whose text is located on the last page, is designed to complement a tape recording of the story by Donna Lanette Washington. It is about Shalesea, the best double-dutcher in the whole school, and Mayvelline, a transfer student who claims to have been the best double-dutcher at her old school. Mayvelline challenges Shalesea to a game, telling her that she cannot wear the shoes she has had since kindergarten. Mayvelline thinks the shoes are what makes Shalesea so good. This story of urban children is a good book for introducing the game of double-dutch.

Ringgold, Faith. (1991). *Tar Beach*. New York: Crown Publishers. Grades K–2.

Tar beach, the roof of the apartment building where eight-year-old Cassie lives, is a center for family activities. From the roof, Cassie is able to fly and help her family with their financial worries. Very colorful illustrations and text show a wonderful African American family enjoying life, friends, and each other without material wealth.

Steptoe, John. (1987). *Mufaro's Beautiful Daughters: An African Tale.*
New York: Lothrop, Lee, & Shepard Books. Grades 3–5.

This story comes from the people near the Zimbabwe ruins, once a
thriving trading city built by Africans. Mufaro's two daughters, Manyara
and Nyasha, are beautiful, but Manyara is selfish and greedy while
Nyasha is considerate and kind. When the King calls all the maidens
together to choose a wife from among them, Manyara goes to the city
the night before so she will be chosen. Steptoe's lifelike illustrations
paint a beautiful picture of the Zimbabwe land and its inhabitants.

AFRICAN AMERICANS TO REMEMBER

The contributions of African Americans have not been included in many
American history textbooks. Although our textbooks are now making great
strides in this area, a major problem historians face is that there is a
scarcity of information about many important African Americans.

Nevertheless, African Americans such as Crispus Attucks, the first
martyr of the American Revolution, have been involved in the fight for
liberty and justice for as long as the United States has existed. We must
also begin to include the names of African Americans such as Benjamin Banneker, a mathematician and surveyor, along with those of
Washington and Jefferson when we teach about Colonial America.
When our history books omit the names and contributions of such
great inventors as Granville T. Woods, who owned over 60 patents in
the field of electricity, and Lewis Howard Latimer, the only African
American member of the Edison Pioneers (who worked with Edison in
the development of the incandescent light), a great disservice to history
is done. The contributions of African Americans and other people of
color must be shared with all our children if we are to represent the
pluralistic nature of our society as a strength rather than a weakness.
Other African Americans have made significant contributions in science, education, exploration, sports, and other fields. The following
books describe the lives of African American men and women who
have helped make the world and the United States a better place in
which to live.

Altman, Susan. (1989). *Extraordinary Black Americans: From Colonial
to Contemporary Times.* Chicago: Children's Press. Grades 6–8.

Biographies of 85 black men and women who have made a contribution to the United States are contained in this book. The first biography is that of Estavanico, an African who came to America as a
Spanish slave; the final biography is that of Jesse Jackson, the civil
rights leader who tried to win the Democratic nomination for president in 1984. Black and white photographs or illustrations are used
throughout this well-written and informative book.

Brenner, Richard J. (1992). *Michael Jordan.* Syosset, NY: East End Publishing. Grades K–2.

Michael "Air" Jordan, the greatest basketball player in the world, was excluded from his high school basketball team the first two times he tried out. But Jordan never gave up. This easy-to-read book contains color photographs of Jordan on the basketball court as well as on the golf course and taking batting practice.

Connell, Kate. (1993). *Tales from the Underground Railroad.* Austin, TX: Steck-Vaughn Company. Grades 3–5.

A collection of stories about how slaves fleeing the Southern slave states reached the North with the help of sympathizers. The stories of people who formed the Underground Railroad, a series of stops where runaway slaves received aid on their journey to freedom, are told in the book. The personal stories of slaves and of their quest for freedom are also included. The book's human-interest stories, will appeal to children. Black-and-white illustrations are by Debbie Heller.

Davis, Burke. (1976). *Black Heroes of the American Revolution.* New York: Harcourt Brace Jovanovich. Grades 6–8.

In this book, a few of the estimated 5,000 African Americans who fought in the American Revolution are discussed. Some of these individuals, are remembered only by their first name, but they become real as we read of their heroism. These African Americans, many of whom were slaves, could only dream of their own freedom as they strived to win America's independence from the British.

Everston, Jonathan. (1991). *Colin Powell.* New York: Bantam. Grades 3–5.

As Chairman of the Joint Chiefs of Staff, General Colin Powell held the highest position in the military. He is best known for his role in the Persian Gulf War. This biography chronicles General Powell's life from his childhood in New York to his accomplishments in the military. Several black and white photographs are used in this well-written book about the first African American to achieve the important position he holds.

Ferris, Jeri. (1989). *Arctic Explorer: The Story of Matthew Henson.* Minneapolis: Carolrhoda Books, Inc. Grades 6–8.

The North Pole is said to have been discovered by Robert Peary on April 6, 1909. What we must emphasize now is that he did not accomplish this great feat without the help of other men. Accompanying Peary were five others: Matthew Henson, an African American who assisted Peary for 22 years, and four native people of the Artic named Ootah, Ooqueah, Egingwah, and Seegloo. This book, which has received several awards as a science and social studies trade book, gives credit to Matt Henson for the discovery. Another biography by Ferris published by Carolrhoda is *Go Free or Die: A Story About Harriet Tubman* (1988), which is appropriate for grades 3–5.

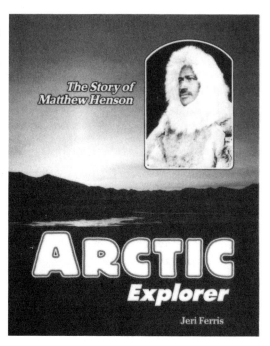

Another book recommended for grades 6–8 is Michael Gilman's *Matthew Henson* (1988), Published by Chelsea House. Gilman effectively portrays this African American's persistence and the disappointments associated with his feat. Another book by Ferris about

FIGURE 4-4 *Arctic Explorer: The Story of Matthew Henson*, by Jeri Ferris. Copyright © 1989 by the author. Published by Carolrhoda Books, Minneapolis.

a notable African American is *What Are You Figuring Now?: A Story about Benjamin Banneker* (1988). Published by Carolrhoda Books, this book tells of how Banneker's accomplishments were used by people who opposed slavery argue that African Americans were as intelligent as whites. Although not rich in African American culture, this book for grades 6–8, gives an interesting account of a famous African American who lived in the late 1700s.

Gause-Jackson, Arlene & Banks-Hayes, Barbara. (1989). *Champions of Change: Biographies of Famous Black Americans.* Austin, TX: Steck-Vaughn Company. Grades 3–5.

Short biographies of ten African Americans are provided in this workbook-type book. Among the better-known subjects are Bill Cosby, the television celebrity; Martin Luther King, Jr., the great civil rights leader; and Jesse Owens, the great Olympic athlete. Also featured are Tom Bradley, former mayor of Los Angeles, and Maya Angelou, the author and poet. At the end of each biography a set of questions is provided to aid in comprehension. Although unattractive in layout, this book with its black-and-white photographs does provide factual and interesting information.

Greenberg, Keith Elliot. (1992). *Magic Johnson: Champion with a Cause.* Minneapolis: Lerner Publications. Grades 6–8.

Earvin "Magic" Johnson retired from professional basketball soon after he found out that he was infected with the human immunodeficiency virus (HIV), which causes AIDS. This book shares Magic Johnson's high and low points on and off the court. Be prepared to discuss sex, because on page 56 Greenberg includes the fact that Magic Johnson, during an interview on the Arsenio Hall Show, urged people to use condoms during sexual intercourse, as well as emphasizing that the only sure way to avoid the HIV virus is to not have sex. Although the reading level is more appropriate for grades 3–5, some might feel that the subject of this book is more appropriate for grades 6–8.

Haber, Louis. (1970). *Black Pioneers of Science and Invention.* New York: Harcourt Brace Jovanovich. Grade 6–8.

This book is a must for information about African Americans who have made significant contributions to the world of science. Seven inventors and seven scientists who were pioneers in their fields are highlighted. The stories of these remarkable men are accompanied by black-and-white photographs or illustrations.

Hamilton, Virginia. (1988). *Anthony Burns: The Defeat and Triumph of a Fugitive Slave.* New York: Alfred A. Knopf. Grades 6–8.

This is an historical account of a runaway slave who made his way to the North only to be imprisoned in Boston under the Fugitive Slave Act of 1850. Hamilton alternates chapters between Burns's experiences and thoughts as a prisoner in a Boston jail awaiting trial and his memories of life as a slave in Virginia. The author has also provided a List of Characters to help sort out the people involved in the story. Hamilton's vivid picture of the cruelty of slavery and of the African Americans who survived this terrible period makes this a good novel for older students.

Haskins, Jim & Benson, Kathleen. (1984). *Space Challenger: The Story of Guion Bluford.* Minneapolis: Carolrhoda Books. Grades 3–5.

This is the authorized biography of the first African American in space, who in 1983 was a member of the crew of the space shuttle Challenger. It gives a chronological account of Bluford's childhood and his eventful days in space as an astronaut. This book is easy to read and should be of interest to those who are fascinated with space travel. Color and black-and-white photographs provide additional information.

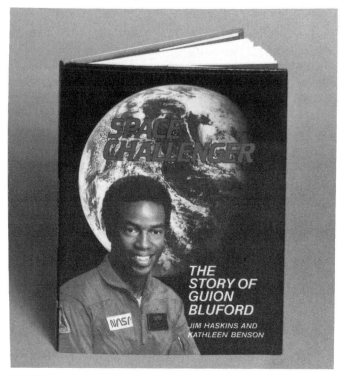

FIGURE 4-5 *Space Challenger: The Story of Guion Bluford*, by Jim Haskins and Kathleen Benson, copyright © 1984 by the authors. Published by Carolrhoda Books, Minneapolis.

Holmes, Mary Z. (1992). *See You In Heaven.* Austin, TX: Steck-Vaughn Company. Grades 6–8.

Although this is not a biography, Holmes' story about life as a slave as seen through the eyes of a young African American in Alabama in 1836 is truly believable. The illustrations by Rick Whipple add to the realism of the story. This book stirs the emotions, and will leave the reader wondering how slavery could ever have existed.

Hart, Philip S. (1992). *Flying Free: America's First Black Aviators.* Minneapolis: Lerner Publications. Grades 3–5.

With the help of black-and-white photographs, the author describes the contributions of African Americans in the field of aviation. Because of segregation and discrimination during the 1920s and 1930s, few African American pilots were able to fly. Others never got the opportunity to learn because neither the U.S. government nor private schools would teach them. Despite these obstacles, some African Americans did become pilots. Hart provides information on four early African

American pioneers of aviation, pilots in World War II, and modern-day pilots. The foreword is by Charles Lindbergh's son, Reeve Lindbergh.

Kelso, Richard. (1993). *Building a Dream: Mary Bethune's School.* Austin, TX: Steck-Vaughn Company. Grades 3–5.

Mary Bethune was the only one of 15 brothers and sisters to have the opportunity to go to school in South Carolina. A school for African American children had opened "just five

FIGURE 4-6 *Flying Free: America's First Black Aviators* by Philip S. Hart. Text copyright 1992 by the author. Published by Lerner Publications Company, Minneapolis.

miles away." She later went to a school in North Carolina that trained her to be a teacher. This well written story describes Mary Bethune's determination to open a school for African American girls in Florida. Starting with $1.50 in her purse, she eventually built a school that today is a college for about 2,300 students.

Other titles in the Stories of America series depicting the lives of African Americans are Richard Kelso's *Walking for Freedom: The Montgomery Bus Boycott* (1993) and *Days of Courage: The Little Rock Story* (1993), and Walter Dean Myers's *A Place Called Heartbreak: A Story of Vietnam* (1993).

Lowery, Linda. (1987). *Martin Luther King Day.* New York: Scholastic. Grades: K–2.

No African American is as well known throughout the world as Dr. Martin Luther King, Jr. Several children's books have been written about Dr. King since his assassination in April of 1968 in Tennessee. This book, with color illustrations, is especially valuable because it not only introduces children to Dr. King and the struggle for equality by African Americans, but also provides the history of the creation of the national holiday in honor of his birthday.

Other books for K–2 children are Walter Dean Myers's *Young Martin's Promise* (1993), published by Steck-Vaughn, and James T. de Kay's *Meet Martin Luther King, Jr.* (1989), published by Random House. Carol Greene's *Martin Luther King Jr.: A Man Who Changed Things* (1989), published by Children's Press, is appropriate for grades 3-5. For older children (grades 6–8), the following two books are suggested: Jean Darby's *Martin Luther King, Jr.* (1990), published by Lerner Publications Company, and James Haskins's *The Life And Times of Martin Luther King, Jr.* (1977), published by Lothrop, Lee, and Shepard Company.

McKissack, Patricia C. & McKissack, Fredrick. (1990). *James Weldon Johnson: Lift Every Voice and Sing.* Chicago: Children's Book Press. Grades K–2.

James Weldon Johnson and his brother composed the song "Lift Every Voice and Sing," which is now referred to as the "Negro national anthem." Johnson was a very talented man who helped his people as an educator, a lawyer, a writer, a diplomat, and a civil rights leader. This informative biography of one of the great leaders in the history of African Americans includes black-and-white photographs of Johnson as a child and young man. The authors have written a simple story highlighting one man's contribution to the advancement of African Americans.

McKissack, Patricia C. (1984). *Paul Laurence Dunbar: A Poet to Remember.* Chicago: Children's Book Press. Grades 6–8.

Paul Laurence Dunbar was a playwright, novelist, and poet whose work inspired people in the late 1800s. His poems, many of which were written in black dialect or slave talk, stirred much controversy. Some thought they were demeaning, while others viewed them as Dunbar did, as part of the African American experience. This book contains several of his poems as well as details of his life from infancy until his death at age 33.

Medearis, Angela S. (1991). *Dancing With The Indians.* New York: Holiday House. Grades K–2.

With the help of colorful illustrations by Samuel Byrd, Medearis tells the story of a young African American girl's experiences at a Native American powwow in Oklahoma. The Seminole tribe in Florida adopted slaves who had escaped from plantations in the South. When the Seminoles were forced to move to Indian Territory (in present-day Oklahoma), many African Americans made the journey with them. Medearis includes historical information based on the life of her own great-grandfather, John Davis, who lived with the Seminoles for some time. Other books by Medearis that concern the African American experience are *Come This Far To Freedom: A History of African Americans in the United States* (1993, Macmillan); Annie's Gifts (1993, Justus Books); *Louis Armstrong and the Jazz Band: The Story of Louis Armstrong* (1993; Lodestar/Penguin U.S.A.); and *Dare To Dream: The Story of Coretta Scott King* (1993, Lodestar/Penguin U.S.A.).

Medearis, Angela S. (1992). *The Zebra-Riding Cowboy: A Folk Song From the Old West.* New York: Henry Holt & Company. Grades K–2.

The contributions of the African American cowboy have been grossly understated until recently. Medearis offers the tale of an educated newcomer whom the ranch hands presume is a greenhorn, or inexperienced cowboy. The bespectacled, citified fellow proves himself to be an excellent horseman. Color illustrations by María Cristina Brusca give a precise picture of cultural diversity among the cowboys of the Southwest. This humorous, poetic retelling of an old cowboy tale will be a favorite of children who love cowboy stories. The last two pages of the book contain information on African American and Mexican American cowboys.

Silver Burdett has published *Reflections of a Black Cowboy: Book One, Cowboys* (1991) *Book Two, The Buffalo Soldiers* (1991), *Book Three: Pioneers* (1991), and *Book Four: Mountain Men* (1992) by Robert H. Miller. These books, appropriate for grades 3-5, provide historical information on African American contributions in the Old West.

Miller, Dawn M. (1991). *David Robinson: Backboard Admiral.* Minneapolis: Lerner Publications. Grade 3-5.

David Robinson, a graduate of the U.S. Naval Academy, began his professional basketball career with the San Antonio Spurs in 1989. This book gives an account of his days at the Naval Academy and his rise to fame as a basketball player. Lerner Publications has several titles about other African American sports heroes that are also well written and entertaining. They are *Florence Griffith Joyner: Dazzling Olympian* (1989) by Nathan Aaseng, *Dwight Gooden: Strikeout King* (1988) by Nathan Aaseng, and *Michael Jordan: Basketball's Soaring Star* (1988) by Paul J. Deegan.

Mitchell, Barbara. (1986). *Shoes for Everyone: A Story about Jan Matzeliger*. Minneapolis: Carolrhoda Books. Grades 3–5.

A young immigrant from Dutch Guiana, Jan Matzeliger invented a shoe-making machine in the 1880s that revolutionized the shoe industry. His shoe-lasting machine, which connected the upper part of the shoe to the inner sole, turned out 700 pairs of shoes in a 10-hour day compared to the 50 pairs turned out by one worker. Because of the increased production, Matzeliger's invention made shoes more affordable. Unfortunately, Matzelinger was all but forgotten because he was forced to give up his patent in order to obtain funds to manufacture his invention. This book will be a tremendous inspiration for African American children relating to Matzeliger's struggles.

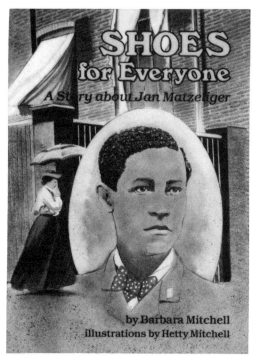

FIGURE 4-7 *Shoes for Everyone: A Story about Jan Matzeliger*, by Barbara Mitchell. Illustrations by Hetty Mitchell. Text copyright © 1986 by the author. Published and illustrated by Carolrhoda Books, Inc., Minneapolis.

Myers, Walter Dean. (1993). *Malcolm X: By Any Means Necessary*. New York: Scholastic. Grades 6–8.

This biography is an interesting look at one of the most important and controversial men in the African American community. Myers shows young people the transformation of Malcolm Little into the man the world would come to know as Malcolm X. This book is well written and provides insight into the African American experience. For example, Myers explains that former slaves retained the surname of their owners in order to locate loved ones who had been sold and taken to other parts of the South. This information allows the reader to better understand Malcolm X's desire to free himself of his surname. This is an excellent book for older students.

O'Connor, Jim. (1989). *Jackie Robinson and the Story of All-Black Baseball*. New York: Random House. Grades 3–5.

Several books have been written about Jackie Robinson, the first African American to play baseball in the major leagues. What makes this book unique is that it introduces us to the professional all-black Negro Leagues. The colorful stories about some of the legends of the all-black teams, such as Rube Foster, Satchel Paige, Josh Gibson, and others, are told in a way that even non-baseball fans will enjoy.

Reef, Catherine. (1993). *Buffalo Soldiers.* New York: Macmillan. Grades 3–5.

Using photographs of African American soldiers in the Old West, this book describes the contributions of the "buffalo soldiers," so named by the Native Americans, who said that their black faces peering through their buffalo coats made them resemble buffaloes.

REFERENCES

Haber, Louis. (1970). *Black pioneers of science and invention.* New York: Harcourt Brace Jovanovich.

Hamilton, Virginia. (1987). The known, the remembered, and the imagined: Celebrating Afro-American folktales. *Children's Literature in Education, 18,* pp. 66-75.

Kantrowitz, Barbara, & Wiley, Constance. (1988, January). The joys of Kwanzaa. *Newsweek,* p. 63.

Hoffman, A., Payne, S., & Smith, R. United States: African Americans. In Miller-Lachmann, L. (1992). *Our family, our friends, our world: An annotated guide to significant multicultural books for children and teenagers.* New Providence, NJ: R. R. Bowker.

Osa, Osayimwense. (1985). The rise of African children's literature. *The Reading Teacher, 38,* pp. 750-754.

Swanson, B. (1992). *Spice up the melting pot: What's new in multicultural literature, grades 4-8.* Paper presented at the 1992 Texas State Reading Association Conference.

5

BOOKS FOR AND ABOUT CHINESE AMERICANS, JAPANESE AMERICANS, AND OTHER ASIAN AMERICANS

Asian Americans are a diverse cultural entity in that they represent various ethnic, national, and racial groups (Worsnop, 1991). According to the 1990 Census, the Asian American community makes up 2.9 percent of the total population. Chinese Americans are the largest Asian population in the United States, but the Asian American mosaic also includes Filipino Americans (19 percent of the Asian American population), Japanese Americans (12 percent), Indian Americans (11 percent), Korean Americans (11 percent), Vietnamese Americans (8 percent), and a smaller percentage from other Asian countries.

Asian Americans also speak various languages, each of which has its own alphabet (Worsnop, 1991). Therefore, there is a need for a variety of books that will provide a better awareness of the similarities and differences among the various Asian populations residing in the United States. Many of these similarites and differences can be seen in folktales. Folktales provide readers with valuable cultural information about specific Asian groups. They are a vital part of the legacy of any culture.

For example, Cathy Spagnoli's *Judge Rabbit and the Tree Spirit* (1991) is a Cambodian story that teaches young children to be confident, and kind to others, and be willing to help others. Judge Rabbit stories are told to teach Cambodian values.

While most folktales do not have contemporary settings, it is important to explain that these stories reflect an ancient lifestyle which may not accurately depict contemporary Asian people (Chu & Schuler, 1992). Stories with Asian American characters who live in contemporary homes and wear fashionable clothes and hairstyles that also show aspects of their specific cultures are valuable. Such books are useful in encouraging children to examine current issues of relevance to Japanese Americans, Korean Americans, and other Asian Americans. For example, in Jayne Pettit's (1992) *My Name Is San Ho* a Vietnamese immigrant to the United States shares his feelings while attempting to adjust to an American school and culture. The story concerns issues of relevance to immigrants of Vietnamese ancestry as well other Asian American children who are new to this country.

Other books allow children to learn about the differences among several Asian American communities in terms of a common theme. *Dara's Cambodian New Year* (1992), *Chinese New Year's Dragon* (1992), and *Tet: The New Year* (1992) describe customs and traditions involved in the celebration of this important spring holiday by different Asian American cultures.

Asian Americans have contributed to the growth of North America for over 150 years (Aoki, 1981). Nonetheless, stereotypes and misinformation about Asian Americans persist. Lewis (1992) cautions that some books depicting Asian Americans contain inaccurate information or are carelessly illustrated. For example, books, which highlight various nations around the world, may be written by people who may never have been to that country or may have researched it inadequately. Also, illustrations are very important and should be examined for accurate depiction of Asian cultures.

Children should have the opportunity to learn more about the history and contributions, as well as the cuisine, art, and literature of Chinese Americans, Japanese Americans, Filipino Americans, and other Asian Americans. With this goal in mind, the books in this chapter are divided in three categories: Chinese American Children's Literature, Japanese American Children's Literature and Books About Other Asian Americans. Books listed in the first section provide insight into Chinese and Chinese American culture. The titles listed in the second section provide information about Japanese Americans. The third section provide information on Filipino Americans, Korean Americans, Vietnamese Americans, and other Asian Americans.

CHINESE AMERICAN CHILDREN'S LITERATURE

According to the 1990 U.S. Census, Chinese Americans are the largest group of Asian Americans in the United States accounting for about 23 percent of the Asian American population. As a group Chinese Americans makeup 0.7 percent of the American population with 1.6 million people. A large percentage of Chinese Americans are foreign-born and still in the process of acculturating and assimilating into mainstream American culture (Huang, & Ying, 1989).

In Chapter 2, *The Five Chinese Brothers* was cited as an example of a book that employs stereotypes, since the Chinese in the story are depicted *as all looking alike*. Although the story is appealing, the images it leaves in the minds of children do not justify its use (Aoki, 1981). Mahy's (1990) book *The Seven Chinese Brothers* is just as entertaining as the *The Five Chinese Brothers*, but far more accurate in its depiction of Chinese culture. The watercolor illustrations by Jean and Mou-sien Tseng draw on careful research. The following books are also noteworthy for their accurate depiction of the various aspects of Chinese culture and the emerging Chinese American culture.

Mahy, Margaret. (1990). *The Seven Chinese Brothers*. New York: Scholastic. Grades 3–5.

Mahy tells the classic Chinese folktale of seven brothers and their supernatural gifts. Thanks to the strong brotherly love that exists among them, the seven brothers are able to endure the hardships that befall their family. The story with its captivating watercolor illustrations by Jean and Mou-sien Tseng, will entertain children.

FIGURE 5-1 *Yang the Youngest and His Terrible Ear* by Lensey Namioka. Copyright © 1992 by Little, Brown and Company. Reprinted by permission of Little, Brown and Company.

Namioka, Lensey. (1992). *Yang the Youngest and His Terrible Ear*. Boston: Little, Brown and Company. Grades 6–8.

When his family immigrates from China to Seattle, Washington, Yingtao must help his father attract students to his private music lessons. References to Chinese culture are dispersed throughout the story. For example, as the youngest Yang, Yintao is not allowed to call his older brother and sisters by their given names. He must refer to them as Eldest Brother, Second Sister, and Third Sister. He is called Fourth Brother by his siblings. Namioka tells an entertaining and humorous story of a young immigrant child with a tin ear who strives to express his individuality in a family of talented musicians. Although the story lacks vivid descriptions of the culture shock experienced by most immigrants, it does provide glimpses of some of the adjustments that America's newest arrivals must make.

Say, Allen. (1990). *El Chino*. Boston: Houghton Mifflin Company. Grades 3–5.

This is the story of *El Chino*, the first bullfighter of Chinese descent. As a young boy from Nogales, Arizona, Bong Way Wong longs to become a professional basketball player but because of his small stature, he is not able to play at the university level. Even after he earns a college degree in engineering, Billy (as his brothers and sisters call him) longs for the limelight. Later, on a trip to Spain, he is introduced to the art of bullfighting and realizes that he is well

FIGURE 5-2 *Chinese New Year's Dragon* by Rachel Sing. © 1992 by The Children's Museum, Boston. Cover reprinted by permission of Modern Curriculum Press.

suited to this art form. However, he is told that only Spaniards can be true matadors. The watercolor illustrations and black-and-white illustrations make this book a photo essay. It is an informative story about an individual who through determination and hard work achieves his goals.

Sing, Rachel. (1992). *Chinese New Year's Dragon.* Cleveland, OH: Modern Curriculum Press. Grades K–2.

The traditions surrounding the celebration of the Chinese New Year are seen through the eyes of a young Chinese American girl. The girl's mother, Nainai, and her Aunt Wang prepare the traditional dishes to be served on New Year's Eve. Readers will enjoy the color illustrations by Shao Wei Liu of a family preparing for a holiday, and of the young girl's fantasy of riding the Chinese Lunar Year dragon. Photographs are used to show a Chinese New Year calendar, a Chinese market, traditional Chinese envelopes, and a parade dragon. From the Multicultural Celebrations series, this book contains a glossary of six Chinese words used in the story.

Stock, Catherine. (1984). *Emma's Dragon Hunt.* New York: Lothrop, Lee, & Shepard Books. Grades K–2.

Emma is a Chinese American girl who is excited that her Grandfather Wong has come from China to live with her family. When Grandfather tells the family that their house will attract Chinese dragons, Emma is frightened. As Grandfather Wong and Emma spend the next two days searching for dragons, he teaches that they are responsible for natural phenomena such as earthquakes, thunderstorms, heat waves, and solar eclipses. The color illustrations by the author while showing people of Chinese ancestory dressing, eating, and living like North Americans introduce Chinese culture. The loving relationship between a grandfather and his grandchild is another strong feature of this story.

Tompart, Ann. (1990). *Grandfather Tang's Story.* New York: Crown Publishers. Grades K–2.

Grandfather Tang and Little Soo use tangrams, ancient Chinese puzzles, to tell a story of fox fairies, supernatural creatures with amazing powers. Grandfather Tang and Little Soo's story has the two fairy foxes changing into the shapes of various animals as they chase each other. The story is entertaining and the tangrams adding a unique feature. The last page of the book provides more information on tangrams and a tangram pattern to trace and cut out.

Waters, Katie & Slovenz-Low, Madeline. (1990). *Lion Dancer: Ernie Wan's Chinese New Year.* New York: Scholastic. Grades K–2.

This photo essay of six-year-old Ernie Wan provides the reader with an enlightening look at one family's celebration of the Chinese New Year.

With over 40 color photographs, the book provides a panorama of the life for a Chinese American family living in New York. Explanations of the Chinese lunar calendar and of the Chinese horoscope are provided at the end of the book. Children will enjoy celebrating this spring festival with Ernie Wan.

Yee, Paul. (1990). *Tales from Gold Mountain: Stories of the Chinese in the New World.* New York: Macmillan. Grades 6–8.

Gold Mountain is the term that the first Chinese immigrants used to refer to North America. Chinese men left their homeland to find their fortune on Gold Mountain and eventually sent for their families. Unfortunately, the hard work they left behind in the fields of China was replaced by work on the railroads and in the goldmines. Very few of the Chinese newcomers made a fortune in North America. These eight stories tell of the hardship, tragedy, and romance of the first Chinese immigrants to North America. Each story is accompanied by a richly colored illustration by Simon Ng Yee, a third-generation Chinese Canadian, providing a vivid look at a group of people whose contributions to North America have yet to be fully appreciated.

Yen, Clara. (1991). *Why Rat Comes First.* San Francisco: Children's Book Press. Grades 3–5.

Jade King, king of all creation, invited all the birds, fish, and other animals of the earth to a great feast. Expecting to see thousands of animals enter heaven's gate, the King was very upset when only 12 animals arrived at the feast. Not wanting to disappoint his guests, he cheerfully announced that the 12 animals would be honored by having the 12 years in the calendar cycle named after them. But who would come first? With Rat and Ox both arguing that he deserved to be first, the King asked the other animals present to decide. When they couldn't decide, Jade King ordered the children of the world to make the decision. Two pages at the end of the book provide information on the Chinese lunar calendar. The color illustrations by Hideo C. Yoshida of the comical animal characters are a principal feature of this story.

Yep, Laurence. (1989). *The Rainbow People.* New York: HarperCollins. Grades 6–8.

This collection of 26 stories from the 1930s provides insight into the culture and the experiences of the Chinese Americans who migrated to the northern part of California. Yep has organized the stories according to five traditional Chinese themes: *Tricksters, Fools, Virtues and Vices, in Chinese America, and Love.* Each one is introduced by the author with a short essay.

Other titles written by this notable Chinese American author, appropriate for grades 6-8 and published by Harper & Row, include *Sweetwater* (1983), a science fiction story about a boy and a group of people attempting to preserve their way of life on another planet; *Dragon of the Lost Sea* (1982), a Chinese myth of a dragon princess, who with the help of a human boy, attempts to capture a witch; *Sea Glass* (1979), a contemporary story of 13-year-old Craig Chin, who has difficulty finding the balance between being American and being Chinese; *Child of the Owl* (1977), a contemporary story whose 12-year-old Chinese American protagonist was raised by her father on the road and has problems adjusting to life in Chinatown; and *Dragonwings* (1979), a fantasy set in the 1900s in San Francisco's Chinatown about a Chinese American father who dreams of again becoming a Chinese dragon and of his son Moonshadow, who helps him pursue his dream of flying.

Yep, Laurence. (1991). *The Star Fisher.* New York: Morrow Junior Books. Grades 6–8.

Fifteen-year-old (16 years old if like the Chinese you count the year in the womb) moves with her parents and two siblings from Ohio to West Virginia to open a laundry in the late 1920s. In China her father was a scholar and a poet, but in order to make a living in North America he must wash and iron clothes. Yep's readable style allows readers to become involved in the situations that confront a Chinese American family as they strive to become a part of the American mosaic. This sensitive story's memorable characters also provide insight into the conflicts of white Americans as they debate whether to acceptance or rejection the new family.

Young, Ed. (1989). *Lon Po Po: A Red-Riding Hood Story from China.* New York: Scholastic. Grades K–2.

Three children are left home alone. Despite instructions to lock the door come evening, the children are tricked into unlocking the door by a wolf impersonating their grandmother. Based on an ancient folktale, the story recounts the children's attempt to escape from the wolf. Children will enjoy the story's action as well as its conclusion. Young's watercolor and pastel illustrations capture the suspenseful mood.

BOOKS ABOUT JAPANESE AMERICANS

According to the 1970 Census, Japanese Americans were the largest Asian American population in the United States. As of 1990, the Japanese American population is the third largest after Chinese Americans and Filipino Americans. Unlike Chinese Americans, less than 30 percent of Japanese Americans are foreign-born (Nagata, 1989). By the year 2000, the Japanese American population is estimated to drop to 8.7 percent of the Asian American population (Gardner, Robey, & Smith, 1985).

Although Japanese Americans are only the third largest Asian American group, there are far more children's books about them than about Filipino Americans. Lewis (1992) states that some of the books about Japanese Americans contain inaccurate information. Lewis cites Arlene Mosel and Blair Lent's (1972) *Funny Little Woman*, Anita Lobel's (1991) *Dwarf Giant*, and Tony Johnston's (1990) *Badger and the Magic Fan* with drawings by Tomie dePaola as picture books containing inaccurate illustrations. Illustrations in the first book depict characters wearing *kimonos*, the traditional robe worn by people of Japanese ancestry, in a way that is reserved for the deceased. The second book shows chopsticks in hair, and the third shows food being served in a manner reserved for dead ancestors. Lewis suggests that such minor flaws should be discussed to help students get a better understanding of people and their culture, but major flaws should not be tolerated. The following books will provide readers with a better understanding of the Japanese Americans.

Chin, Steven A. (1993). *When Justice Failed: The Fred Korematsu Story.* Austin, TX: Steck-Vaughn Company. Grades 6–8.

Toyosaburo "Fred" Korematsu, a *Nisei* (a first-generation Japanese American), was born in Oakland, California. As an American of Japanese descent, life was difficult for him and others like him before and after the Japanese attacked Pearl Harbor. He was not allowed to enlist in the armed forces and he lost his job as a welder in the shipyard. With the signing of Executive Order 9066 by President Roosevelt, people of Japanese ancestry were forced to move within one week's time to an internment camp. This well-written story focuses on the *test case* of the constitutionality of the imprisonment of Japanese Americans during World War II. Black and white photographs are included, and the author's descriptions of Fred's experiences paint a vivid picture for the reader. This is a very special book that will enable children to understand the injustice and pain experienced by Japanese Americans.

Christopher, Matt. (1988). *Shortstop from Tokyo*. New York: Little, Brown and Company. Grades 6–8.

With exciting play-by-play accounts of baseball games, Christopher tells the story of Hideko (Sam) Suzuki, an immigrant Japanese boy who plays shortstop for the Mohawks. Sam begins to compete with another boy, Stogie, for the same position, and when Stogie allows his favorite glove to be chewed up by a wild animal, Sam sees it as revenge.

Sam has been in the United States for only one or two years with his father, a visting professor, but very little is said about Japanese culture. Originally written in 1970, this book gives Japanese American children a fictional character with whom they can relate.

Morimoto, Junko. (1986). *The Inch Boy.* New York: Penguin Books. Grades K–2.

An old couple pray to Buddha for a son. One day, they find a one-inch-long boy, Issunboshi, on their doorstep. He becomes a loyal follower of the great Lord Sanjo, an honorable man. On his first day on duty, Issunboshi must save the princess from a giant. Loyalty and re-

FIGURE 5-3 *Shortstop From Tokyo* by Matt Christopher. Copyright © 1988 by Little, Brown and Company (Inc.). Reprinted by permission of Little, Brown and Company.

spect for one's elders are two values expressed in this Japanese Tom Thumb story. This book, beautifully illustrated by the author, captures the brave actions of this minute hero.

Sakai, Kimiko. (1990). *Sachiko Means Happiness.* San Francisco: Children's Book Press. Grades K–2.

Five-year-old Sachiko has seen her grandmother change with Alzheimer's disease, and her confused state is frightening. Sachiko

FIGURE 5-4 *Sachiko Means Happiness* by Kimiko Sakai, copyright © 1990 by Children's Book Press. Reprinted by permission of Bookstop Literacy Agency, Agent for Children's Book Press.

sees her grandmother cry and realizes that she feels herself to be a little girl. In Japanese tradition, grandparents name their grandchildren and part of the story is that Sachiko's name was given to her by her grandmother. The vivid pastel illustrations are by Tomie Arai.

Yashima, Taro. (1958). *Umbrella.* New York: Viking. Grades K–2.

Yoko has received an umbrella and boots for her birthday. Unfortunately, the little girl must wait for a rainy day before she can use them. Children will be able to relate to Yoko as she comes up with different ideas for getting permission to use the umbrella. Japanese characters and words for spring, summer, rain, and peach are included. The oldest book listed in this chapter, *Umbrella* continues to entertain children.

BOOKS ABOUT OTHER ASIAN AMERICANS

According to Chu and Schuler (1992) there remains a major gap in the number of children's books for and about Filipino Americans, Asian Indian Americans, and Pakistani Americans. Our hope is that the quantity (and quality) of books for these and other Asian Americans will increase. The following books are suggested as excellent resources to help Asian American children see themselves in the literature, and to help other children gain a better understanding of Korean Americans, Filipino Americans, and other Asian American cultures. Each entry will indicate in parentheses the Asian American group that the story concerns.

FIGURE 5-5 *Dara's Cambodian New Year* by Sothea Chiemroum. © 1992 by The Children's Museum, Boston. Cover reprinted by permission of Modern Curriculum Press, Inc.

Chiemroum, Sothea. (1992). *Dara's Cambodian New Year*. Cleveland, OH: Modern Curriculum Press. Grades 3–5. (Cambodian American)

As a Cambodian American family prepares to celebrate its second Cambodian New Year in the United States, the grandparents are homesick for Cambodia. Although their grandson Dara has become Americanized, he feels sad to see his grandparents so upset. Through his artwork, Dara is able to help cheer them up. A glossary at the end of the book provides the pronunciation of Cambodian words used. Color illustrations by Dam Nang Pin and photographs provide a glimpse of life in Cambodia, in a Cambodian community in the United States, and during the three-day Cambodian New Year celebration. The two-page picture of the Cambodian countryside is spectacular.

Gilson, Jamie. (1985). *Hello, My Name is Scrambled Eggs*. New York: Lothrop, Lee & Shepard Books. Grades 6–8. (Vietnamese American)

Harvey Trumble is a teenager who sees an opportunity to have "a kid of his own" when he finds out that a church-sponsored Vietnamese family coming to live with his family has a boy about his age. Unfortunately for Harvey, Tuan Nguyen has a mind of his own. An added problem for Harvey is the prejudice of his friend, Quint, against Tuan Nguyen and his family. As the story proceeds, Quint begins to befriend the young Vietnamese American boy who is learning to be an American but continues to hold onto his Vietnamese culture. This is a good book for introducing Vietnamese culture and some of the hardships experienced by new immigrants.

Kim-Lan Tran. (1992). *Têt: The New Year*. Cleveland, OH: Modern Curriculum Press. Grades K–2. (Vietnamese American)

FIGURE 5-6 *Têt: The New Year* by Kim-Lan Tran. © 1992 by The Children's Museum, Boston. Cover reprinted by permission of Modern Curriculum Press.

This book provides an informative look at the three-day celebration of the Vietnamese New Year. Written under the auspices of The Children's Museum in Boston, this book is from the series, "Multicultural Celebrations"

FIGURE 5-7 *Aekyung's Dream* by Min Paek, copyright © 1988 by Children's Book Press. Reprinted by permission of Bookstop Literacy Agency, Agent for Children's Book Press.

which highlights holidays celebrated by American people of color. The glossary with pronunciations for the Vietnamese words used in the story is printed in the back. The illustrations, by the award-winning artist Vo-Dinh Mai, and color photographs are helpful in explaining this Vietnamese holiday.

Lee, Jeanne M. (1987). *Ba-Nam.* New York: Henry Holt & Company. Grades K–2. (Vietnamese American)

This simple story of a young girl's visit with her family to the graves of their ancestors is based on the author's childhood experiences in South Vietnam. In Vietnamese tradition, Thanh-Minh Day is when families present gifts to their ancestors. In this story, Nan, a young girl, meets an old woman who is the keeper of the graves. Nan is afraid of the old woman, Ba-Nam, because of her appearance, but soon finds out that she is a good person. This is a good story for teaching about the dangers of prejudging people based on their appearance.

Mayberry, Jodine. (1990). *Filipinos.* New York: Franklin Watts. Grades 6–8. (Filipino American)

An introduction to Filipino culture, this book is from Recent Immigrants series. Black-and-white and color photographs, maps, and charts teach the reader about the migration of Filipinos to the United States. The book also focuses on the contributions of Filipinos to North America, and may be used as a resource when studying the second-largest Asian American group in the United States.

Paek, Min. (1988). *Aekyung's Dream.* San Francisco: Children's Book Press. Grades K–2. (Korean American)

Aekyung is a young Korean American girl who learns to adapt to her new life in America by learning about Korean history. Aekyung expresses her alienation and loneliness when she tells her mother that she does not want to go to school. With the help of a dream about King Sejonj, creator of the Korean alphabet, she begins to adjust to her new environment. The simple colored illustrations and English/Korean text make this an excellent book for teaching Korean as well as other children about cultural pride.

Pettit, Jayne. (1992). *My Name is San Ho.* New York: Scholastic. Grades 6–8. (Vietnamese American)

With his mother and North American stepfather, San Ho leaves Vietnam after the war has destroyed their crops and killed their friends and neighbors. Adjusting to their new homeland is made especially difficult when San Ho and his mother realize that not all their new neighbors welcome their presence. This is the story of a 12-year-old boy's experience of racism. San Ho's success on the baseball field provides him with some comfort as he slowly begins to adjust.

Spagnoli, Cathy. (1991). *Judge Rabbit and the Tree Spirit: A Folktale from Cambodia.* San Francisco: Children's Book Press. Grades 3–5. (Cambodian American)

When a young man leaves home to go off to war, a tree spirit disguises himself as the young man and goes to live with his wife. When the young man returns, his wife is unable to tell her real husband from the tree spirit. Judge Rabbit, a wise and helpful creature, offers to help the young man. Written in both English and Khmer, this book provides information about the customs and foods of the Cambodian people. Told by Lina Mao Wall, it is one of many Judge Rabbit stories, and encourages Cambodian and Cambodian American children to be self-confident and wise.

Stern, Jennifer. (1989). *The Filipino Americans.* New York: Chelsea House. Grades 6–8. (Filipino American)

The lifestyle of Filipino Americans is described in this book. Outstanding Filipino Americans are profiled and the history of the Philippines as a Spanish colony, an American colony, and a sovereign nation is included. This is a well-written and interesting book that contains black and white and color photographs.

For grades 3-5, Frank Winter's *Filipinos in America* (1988) provides an informative look at famous Filipinos. It is published by Lerner Publications. These two books are valuable resources for those seeking information on the second-largest Asian American group in the United States.

Surat, Michele Maria. (1983). *Angel Child, Dragon Child.* Milwaukee: Raintree Publishers. Grades K–2. (Vietnamese American)

This story tells of a young Vietnamese girl who is having a difficult time adjusting to her new life in the United States. Ut, as she is called at home, is also sad because her mother

FIGURE 5-8 *Korean Children's Day* by Ruth Suyenaga with Young Sook Kim and Young Mi Pak. © 1992 by The Children's Museum, Boston. Cover reprinted by permission of Modern Curriculum Press, Inc.

is still in Vietnam. The immigrant experience is well expressed in the text and the color-pencil drawings by Vo-Dinh Mai. Pronunciation is provided for the Vietnamese words used in the story. Two pages at the end of the story provide more information about Vietnamese culture.

Suyenaga, R., Young Sook Kim and Young Mi Pak. (1992). *Korean Children's Day.* **Cleveland, OH: Modern Curriculum Press. Grades K–2. (Korean American)**

To show respect, Young Soo Newton and his teacher bow to each other at the Korean Institute. This book introduces readers to the Korean alphabet, to a Korean game called *kut*, to Korean food, and to some of the activities associated with the spring holiday called Korean Children's Day. The glossary at the end of the book provides the pronunciation of Korean words used. Color illustrations by Nani Kyong-Nan and color photographs complement the text. This book is from the Multicultural Celebrations series.

FIGURE 5-9 *The Little Weaver of Thái-Yên Village: Cô Bé Thợ-Dệt Làng Thái-Yên* by Trần-Khánh-Tuyết, copyright © 1987 by Children's Book Press. Reprinted by permission of Bookstop Literacy Agency, Agent for Children's Book Press.

Trân-Khánh-Tuyêt. (1987). *The Little Weaver of Thái-Yên Village: Cô Bé Thọ-Dệt Làng Thái-Yên*, rev. ed. San Francisco: Children's Book Press. Grades K–2. (Vietnamese American)

An injured little girl named Hien is taken from the horrors of the Vietnam War to the United States for medical treatment. She is confused that it was American weapons that killed her mother and grandmother, and yet Americans are now helping her. Slowly she adjusts to life in the United States, and sends blankets to her people in Vietnam. Hien's grandmother taught her to weave on a loom, and now she continues the tradition. Based on the stories of the children who came to San Francisco for medical treatment during the war, this book can help children to understand the horrors of war and the pain of those who left Vietnam after the war ended. With color illustrations by Nancy Hom, the book is written in Vietnamese with an English translation by Christopher N.H. Jenkins and the author. Vietnamese words used in the English text are defined at the bottom of each page.

Xiong, Blia. (1989). *Nine in One, GRR! GRR!* San Francisco: Children's Book Press. (Hmong American)

This folktale from the Hmong mountain people of Laos explains why there are only a few tigers in the world. Tiger goes to the god Shao, who can foretell how many cubs she will have. Shao tells her she will have nine each year if she remembers to say *"nine-in-one,"* but Bird tricks her into saying *"one-in-nine"* so she will have fewer cubs. Hmong folktales and legends have been preserved through the oral tradition and tapestries. Beautiful illustrations resembling these traditional story cloths help tell this simple story.

REFERENCES

Aoki, E. M. (1981). Are you Chinese? Are you Japanese? Or are you just a mixed-up kid? Using Asian American children's literature. *The Reading Teacher, 34*, 382-385.

Chu, E. & Schuler, C. V. (1992). United States: Asian Americans. In Miller-Lachmann, L. (ed.), *Our family, our friends, our world: An annotated guide to significant multicultural books for children and teenagers*. New Providence, NJ: R. R. Bowker.

Gardner, R., Robey, B., & Smith, P. (1985). Asian Americans: Growth, change, and diversity. *Population Bulletin, 40*, 1-43.

Huang, L. N. & Ying, Y. (1989). Chinese American Children and Adolescents. In Gibbs, J. T., Huang, L. N. & Associates (ed.), *Children of color*. San Francisco: Jossey-Bass.

Johnston, T. (1990). *Badger and the magic fan: A Japanese folktale*. New York: Putnam.

Lewis, J. Y. (1992). Japan. *Booklinks*, *1* (4), 24-26.

Lobel, A. (1991). *Dwarf giant*. New York: Holiday House.

Mosel, A & Lent, B. (1972). *Funny little woman*. New York: Dutton.

Nagata, D. K. (1989). Japanese American Children and Adolescents. In Gibbs, J. T., Huang, L. N. & Associates (ed.), *Children of color*. San Francisco: Jossey-Bass.

Worsnop, R. L. (1991, December). Asian Americans. *CQ Researcher*: 947-954. Reprinted in *Social Issues Resources Series*, *1* (30). Boca Raton, FL: Social Issues Resources Series.

6 BOOKS FOR AND ABOUT VARIOUS NATIVE AMERICANS

IMAGES OF NATIVE AMERICANS

Lee Little Soldier (personal communication, February 22, 1991) states that stories dealing with Native Americans must provide the reader with information about the following: historical period, tribal group, and location.

Historical period is important because children need to know whether a story takes place in the 1890s or the 1990s if certain stereotypes are to be eliminated. Byler (1977) expressed concern about the number of books depicting Native Americans as malicious, incompetent, or childlike. More recently, Norton (1991) stated that Native Americans continue to be the subject of stereotyping in children's books. We must examine closely the images of Native Americans that are being communicating to our children. Are we providing them with stories that give more than the tomahawk-and-tipi version of Native American life? Images such as this distort contemporary Native American life, and we must not assume that children automatically know the differences between the experiences of contemporary Native American life and the life of past generations. Little Soldier (1982) described this problem when she wrote, "Most young children . . . seem to have the impression that 'Indians' no longer exist. This fallacy occurs when Native American history is not followed into the twentieth century" (p. 44). This point was made clear to us when we sat in on a presentation to a group of children by a member of the Pawnee tribe. During a short question-and-answer session, children were asking the presenter stereotypic questions such as, "Do you live in a tepee?"

The question that must be asked when using Native American Children's Literature is, "Does the story present information about how the people of an ancient civilization lived or does the story present accurate information about how the descendents of these people in society lived." Only if the answer is "yes" will the reader be able to gain a better understanding of the differences between the cultures and lifestyles of contemporary Native Americans and those of their ancestors.

Some books about Native Americans clearly state the period. Bulla and Syson's *Conquista!* (1978) for example takes place in 1541. Although no tribe is named, the young Native American clearly belongs to one of the tribes of the Great Plains. The story is a creative account of what might have happened when a Native American first encountered the horse, and it would be an excellent book about Native Americans were it not for the fact that they are referred to as "savages" (p. 2). We must be sensitive to the terminology used in books as well as in everyday speech when speaking about Native Americans. Terms such as "savages," "wild Indians," "Injun," and "Honest Injun" are examples of enthnocentrism as well as racism. it is critical that we educate our children to be aware of these attitudes—no matter how subtle they may be.

The terms *American Indian, Native American, Indian,* and *Native people* tend to be used in reference to any indigenous person. Since most Native Americans prefer to be called by their tribal name, these terms should be used only when referring to several tribes at once (Hirschfelder, 1986). Hirschfelder also points out that the European name for a tribe may not be the one the tribe uses. For example, the Sioux, who live in the Upper Midwest, who prefer to call themselves the Lakota, means "allies" in their language. Most Native Americans have names that make some reference to "the People." For example, both the Inuit (the name preferred by the Eskimos) and Diné (the name preferred by the Navajo) mean "the people" (Hirschfelder, 1986). The Chippewa, who live in the Great Lakes area, prefer to call themselves Ojibway meaning "the original people" (Esbensen, 1988).

In addition to the correct terminology to use when referring to Native Americans, children also need to learn about the culture and geographic location of specific tribal groups. This will allow them to recognize the diversity within the Native American population. For example, providing children with geographic, cultural, and historical information about the Diné (Navajo) before they read Byrd Baylor's *Hawk, I'm Your Brother* (1976) will help them to appreciate the culture described in the story. Activities such as locating New Mexico and Arizona on the map or researching the contemporary lifestyle of the Diné will help children who are not Native American or who do not live in the Southwest to appreciate more fully the setting and characters in this story. The use of stories about other Southwestern Native Americans will illustrate the diversity of the Native American people, and encourage an appreciation for that diversity.

Despite the number of tribes, Native Americans do share many beliefs and attitudes. Cullinan (1989) states that "American Indians believe in the wholeness of experience, the interdependence of man and nature, the importance of the quest for love, and the search for one's destiny" (p. 612). These beliefs are expressed in such contemporary stories as Jamake Highwater's *Anpao: An American Indian Odyssey* (1977). This story, a classic that has withstood the test of time, is a cultural journey in which a Native American discovers the relationship between Native people and nature.

DEMOGRAPHIC INFORMATION

Native Americans are the original inhabitants of North America, and their history needs to be told accurately. Anthropologists believe that our indigenous people have been in North America for 30,000 to 60,000 years (Goley, 1992). Once estimated at 10 million, the number of native inhabitants was drastically reduced through the policies of the U.S. government in what some have called cultural genocide (LaFromboise & Low, 1989). The 1990 Census reported the number of Native Americans at approximately 1.98 million, twice as many as in 1970 (LaFromboise & Low, 1989).

There are over 250 different Native America tribes in the United States (Little Soldier, 1992). The Cherokee Nation of Oklahoma, with over 230,000 members is the largest (Goley, 1992). The Diné (Navajo) Nation with over 172,000 members is the second largest.

LITERATURE FOR OR ABOUT NATIVE AMERICANS

Although Native Americans make up only 0.8 percent of the total American population, the collection of multiethnic children's literature would be incomplete without the folklore, poetry, and contemporary stories of our Native people (Cullinan, 1989). This chapter attempts to provide adults with the resources necessary to correct the stereotyped view and preconceived ideas children may have of Native Americans.

Divided into the following two categories: (1) *Historical Settings* and (2) *Contemporary Settings*, this chapter focuses on literature written for or about various tribes of Native Americans. Books listed under the first category provide an annotated bibliography of historical fiction and informational books depicting accurately various tribes of North America in the eighteenth and nineteenth centuries. The second section provides an annotated bibliography of titles focusing on contemporary life within various tribes of Native Americans. If the titles of the books do not specify the tribe that is being written about, we have inserted the name of the Native American group for quick reference.

HISTORICAL SETTINGS

Accorsi, William. (1992). *My Name Is Pocahontas.* New York: Holiday House. Grades K–2. (Algonquin)

Best known for saving the life of the Englishman John Smith, Pocahontas was a caring individual who hoped that all people would live in peace. Accorsi provides a beautifully illustrated account of her life. A glossary at the beginning of the book provides information on the main characters in the story.

FIGURE 6-1 *Baby Rattlesnake* by Te Ata, copyright © 1989 by Children's Book Press. Reprinted by permission of Bookstop Literacy Agency, Agent for Children's Book Press.

Ata, Te. (1989). *Baby Rattlesnake*. San Francisco: Children's Book Press. Grades K-2. (Chickasaw)

Lynn Moroney adapted this story from the renowned Chickasaw storyteller, Te Ata. Te Ata, whose name means "Bearer of the Morning," is over 90 years old and first heard this tale as a child in Oklahoma. The story is about Baby Rattlesnake, who cries constantly because he does not have his rattle. Although everyone believes that Baby Rattlesnake is too young for a rattle, the disgusted elders of the council give him one so they can get some peace and quiet. This tale teaches the valuable lesson that it is important to wait for something until one is ready for it. The color illustrations in southwestern hues by Veg Reisberg complements this story of the consequences of a youth's impatience.

Bernard, Emery. (1993). *Spotted Eagle & Black Crow: A Lakota Legend.* New York: Holiday House. Grades K–2. (Lakota)

An adaptation of a story from the people of the Dakotas, this is the tale of two young men who are in love with the same young woman. Black Crow decides to kill Spotted Eagle so that the young woman, Red Bird, will marry him. Spotted Eagle takes Black Crow to a mountain and leaves him to die in an eagle's nest high on a cliff. Although a little slow in developing, the story has a satisfying ending.

Caduto, Michael J. and Joseph Bruchac. (1989). *Keepers of the Earth: Native American Stories and Environment Activities for Children.* Golden, CO: Fulcrum Publishers. Grades 3–5. (Various tribes)

This unique book includes short Native American and Native Alaskan stories that teach about the relationship between people and nature, as well as hands-on activities to help children understand that relationship. The stories, divided into nine themes such as *Sky, Water,* and *Unity of Earth,* expose the reader to Native American traditions from different parts of North America. The activities are intended to facilitate a holistic, interdisciplinary approach to the study of the various Native American and Alaska Native cultures. They will appeal to children in the primary, intermediate, and upper elementary grades.

   Keepers of the Earth: Native American Stories and Wildlife Activities for Children (1991) is another collection of Native American and Alaska Native stories with hands-on activities published by Fulcrum by the same authors. It provides activities that teach children the importance of wildlife conservation.

Cohlene, Terri. (1990). *Turquoise Boy: A Navajo Legend.* Mahwah, NJ: Watermill Press. Grades 3–5. (Diné)

From the Native American Legend series, this is a legend from the indigenous people of Arizona and New Mexico. Turquoise Boy, saddened by the fact that his people work so hard, seeks the gods' help to make their life easier. After many futile attempts to convince the various gods to help his people, he receives a gift of magnificent creatures—horses. The last few pages are devoted to discussion of Diné history and culture. The story is illustrated by Charles Reasoner with color photographs, black-and-white photographs, and sketches that provide background information on the Diné. Equally strong works with a similar format by the same author and illustrator are *Clamshell: A Makah Legend* (1990), *Dancing Drum: A Cherokee Legend* (1990), *Little Firefly: An Algonquin Legend* (1990), *Ka-Ha-Si and the Loon: An Eskimo Legend* (1990), and *Quillworker: A Cheyenne Legend* (1990).

Erdoes, Rich, and Alfonso Ortiz. (1984). *American Indian Myths and Legends.* New York: Pantheon Books. Grades 6–8. (Various tribes)

Although this 528-page volume may seem more appropriate for adults, many of the tales are less than three pages in length and are suitable for children. The 166 stories reflect the culture of several native people. Answers to the questions of creation are presented in *Part One: Tales of Human Creation* and *Part Two: Tales of World Creation.* Other stories tell of the heavenly bodies, love, monsters, heroes, tricksters, and animals. This collection would serve well as an introduction to the various types of stories told by native Americans. Please note that while most of the stories are suitable for children, a few, such as "Teaching the Mudheads to Copulate," are not.

Esbensen, Barbara J. (1989). *Ladder to the Sky: How the Gift of Healing Came to the Ojibway Nation.* Boston: Little, Brown and Company. Grades K–2. (Ojibway)

FIGURE 6-2 *Ladder to the Sky: How the Gift of Healing came to the Ojibway* by Barbara J. Esbensen. Copyright © 1988 by Little, Brown and Company. Reprinted by permission of Little, Brown and Company.

Long ago the Ojibway were never ill. When someone grew old, the Great Spirit would send a messenger down a magical vine to carry the Old One up into the sky to live forever. No one was allowed to touch this vine. Once a young man was taken by a messenger up to the kingdom, and his grandmother went up the vine in search of him. The vine broke and sent her plummeting back to earth. Disease and death were the people's punishment. Then one day the Great Spirit sent messengers with healing plants and flowers that let the people cure themselves.

Helen Davie's color illustrations incorporate the traditional patterns and motifs of the art of the Ojibway people from the Great Lakes area.

Esbensen, Barbara J. (1988). *The Star Maiden: An Ojibway Tale.* Boston: Little, Brown and Company. Grades K–2. (Ojibway)

This story explains where water lilies come from. Stars came to earth and she tried to live in several places, but they were either too far

FIGURE 6-3 *The Star Maiden: An Ojibway Tale* by Barbara J. Esbensen. Copyright © 1988 by Little, Brown and Company. Reprinted by permission of Little, Brown and Company.

from the people or they were not peaceful. Finally the Star Maiden and her sisters found rest in a dark lake. The next morning the Ojibway saw the water lilies. Esbensen's eloquent and simple words and Helen Davie's exhilarating color illustrations provide a glimpse of Ojibway life. Traditional patterns and motifs of the Ojibway are used in the drawings.

Hayes, Joe. (1990). *A Heart Full of Turquoise: Pueblo Indian Tales.* Santa Fe, NM: Mariposa Publishing. Grades 3–5. (Pueblo)

Joe Hayes, a well-known storyteller from New Mexico, has taken stories from Pueblo tribes such as the Cochiti, Zuni, Tewa, and Taos and adapted them to his storytelling style. Among the 11 stories is a creation story, a teaching tale, a supernatural story, and a Cinderella story.

Another title about Native Americans for young adults from Mariposa Printing & Publishing, a small publishing house established in 1980, is Gerald Hausman's *Ghost Walk: Native American Tales of the Spirit* (1991), a collection of supernatural stories from the Pueblo and Diné people.

Hayes, Joe. (1983). *Coyote &.* **Santa Fe, NM: Mariposa Publishing. Grades 6–8. (Various tribes)**

For many Native Americans in the Southwest, the coyote is an important part of tradition. This collection of "why" stories from various tribes explains why coyotes act and look the way they do. Hayes has written these stories to entertain. With humor and well-defined settings, they are told in the storytelling tradition. The pencil drawings by Lucy Jelinek of coyote and other animals express the humor of the 13 stories.

Highwater, Jamake. (1985). *Eyes of Darkness: A Novel.* **New York: Lothrop, Lee, & Shepard Books. Grades 6–8. (Lakota)**

No bibliography on Native Americans would be complete without some mention of the works of Highwater. In this book he uses the story of Charles Alexander Eastman, a Native American doctor, to convey the beauty in Sioux way of life before the whites took over their lands. Dr. Eastman lives with his people until he is 17 when he is taken to live with the whites. There he becomes a doctor and later returns to work with his people. Highwater's novel shows the pain felt by Dr. Eastman, who, as an educated Lakota, is totally trusted by neither whites nor his own people. Although this is a fictional biography, it provides a memorable Native American character from the late 1800s.

Highwater, Jamake. (1985). *Legend Days.* **New York: Harper & Row. Grades 6–8. (Plains Indians)**

Considered one of the best chroniclers of the Native American experience, Jamake Highwater's books contain memorable characters from the tribes of the Great Plains. The trilogy called *The Ghost Horse Cycle* chronicles the lives of three generations. The first book, *Legend Days* (1984), involves 11-year-old Amana, who is orphaned by a smallpox epidemic and is taken in by grandfather fox. Set in the latter part of the nineteenth century, the story recounts the history of Native Americans from the northern plains during one of their most trying periods.

The Ceremony of Innocence (1985) continues the life of Amana, now a young woman with a fatherless child. Amana attempts to raise her daughter, Jemina, in the ways of her people, but her daughter accepts the white world. Amana becomes more and more disillusioned with the passing years. Jemina grows up to become a wife and mother, but over the years she too comes to be filled with despair and confusion.

The main character of *I Wear the Morning Star* (1986), the final book in the cycle, is Sitko, the grandson of Amana. The setting of the story is southern California in the 1940s and 1950s. Sitko is placed in an orphanage where he is physically and emotionally abused, but as he is growing up, his father, Jamie Ghost Horse, appears to him. Sitko is like his grandmother in being proud of his Plains Indian heritage.

Jumper, Moses, and Ben Sonder. (1993). *Osceola: Patriot and Warrior.* **Austin, TX: Steck-Vaughn Company. Grades 6–8. (Florida Seminole)**

The authors provide a biographical account of the best-known Seminole chief, highlighting his rise to leader. Historical accounts of the Seminole acceptance of runaway slaves as allies are also included. A minor flaw is the lack of Seminole culture in the story. However, the book does show the Seminole love for the land and for their ancestors. Black and white sketches are by Patrick Soper.

Also from the Stories of America series is *These Lands Are Ours: Tecumseh's Fight For the Old Northwest* (1993) by Kate Connell, with illustrations by Jan Naimo Jones. This story is about the Shawnee chief who attempted to unite all the native tribes into a single nation.

Martin, Rafe. (1992). *The Rough-Faced Girl.* **New York: Putman. (Algonquin)**

In a huge wigwam set apart from the rest of the village lived the Invisible Being. Only his sister who lived with him could see him. In this same village lived a man who had three daughters. The two older daughters made the younger daughter care for the campfire. The fire and ashes scarred this girl's face and body, and she was known as "Rough-Faced Girl." The two daughters wanting to marry the rich and powerful Invisible Being were unable to answer the Invisible Being's Sister's questions. The Rough-Faced Girl, laughed at by the people of the village, also approaches the Invisible Being's Sister, wanting to marry the Invisible Being. This "Cinderella" version from the folklore of one of the northeast United States tribes will charm children as it unfolds toward a happy ending. The life-like color illutrations by David Shannon aid in the telling of this story.

Morrow, Mary F. (1992). *Sarah Winnemucca.* **Austin, TX: Steck-Vaughn Company. Grades 3–5. (Paiute)**

One of the most honored Native American women, Sarah Winnemucca fought for fair treatment and a better life for her people. As a member of the Paiute tribe in Nevada, Sarah saw broken treaties, hostile white settlers, and dishonest government agents take advantage of her people. Sarah was fluent in English, and she petitioned different government officials for justice. Unfortunately, during her lifetime, from 1844 to 1891, very few whites cared about the welfare of the native people.

Intermediate-grade readers will appreciate the simple style in which the author tells this story of a woman who spent her entire life attempting to solve the problems of the people she loved. The illustrations are by Ken Bronikowski.

The book and others from the Native American Stories series provide a better understanding of the variety of Native American cultures. Other noteworthy titles about historical figures are *Carlos Montezuma* (1993) by Peter Iverson, the story of a member of the Yavapai of Arizona who earned a medical degree; *Geronimo* (1992) by David Jeffery, about the great Apache chief; *Hole-In-The-Day* (1993) by Robert M. Kvasnicka, the story of one of the chiefs of the Ojibway; *Ishi* (1993) by Louise V. Jeffredo-Warden, the biography of the last surviving member of the Yahi tribe; *John Ross* (1993) by Felix C. Lowe, about the accomplishments and struggles of one of the principal chiefs of the Cherokee; and *Plenty Coups* (1993) by Michael P. Doss, the story of an important Crow chief.

Ortiz, Simon. (1988). *The People Shall Continue*, rev. ed. San Francisco: Children's Book Press. Grades 3–5. (Various tribes)

Originally written in 1977, this revised edition with handwritten text traces the lives and struggles of "the People" from creation to contemporary times. Various Native American creation stories are molded into one at the beginning of the story. As the story recounts how "the People" fought to protect their land and themselves, several Native American leaders are mentioned. At the conclusion of the story, the term "the People" has come to refer to all Americans who have struggled in this country. In the Native American tradition of the teaching story, this book provides historical information as well as the lesson that we are responsible for each other and Mother Earth provides for our needs. The color paintings provide images of historical Native Americans and "the People's" struggles.

Osinski, Alice. (1988). *The Nez Perce*. Chicago: Children's Press. Grades K–2. (Nez Perce)

The Nez Perce call themselves *Nimiipu*, meaning "the real people" (*nez perce* is French for "pierced noses"). This book provides a cultural and historical account of this Native American tribe originally from the states of Utah, Washington, and Oregon. The section entitled "Modern Life" at the end of the book provides text and color photographs of contemporary Nez Perce life. This book is in the New True Books series. Other books in the series with a similar format focus on the Apache, Cherokee, Cheyenne, Chippewa, Choctaw, Eskimos, Hopi, Navajo, Pawnee, Seminole, Shoshone, and Sioux.

Sewall, Marcia. (1990). *People of the Breaking Day.* New York: Antheneum. Grades 3–5. (Wampanoag)

Before the Pilgrims landed at Plymouth Rock, the Wampanoag people lived in the area that became Massachusetts. With illustrations by the author, this book provides a glimpse of what life was like for this Native American tribe in the 1600s. The descriptions of daily tribal and family life are excellent for young children. Two glossaries at the end of the book, one of English words and one of Native American words, are an added feature.

Stein, R. Conrad. (1985). *The Story of The Trail of Tears.* Chicago: Children's Press. Grades 3–5. (Cherokee)

In 1838, the American government began the removal of the Cherokee from their homeland in present-day Georgia. Their trek of almost 1,000 miles from Georgia to Indian Territory (Oklahoma) took six months. One in four Cherokee died on the journey that they called *Nunna-da-ul-tsun-yi* (the place where they cried).

In *The Story of Wounded Knee* (1983), the same author recounts the story of the slaughter of over 200 Sioux in South Dakota in 1890. Although some might argue that children should not be exposed to such stories, we believe that these events must be taught if children are to understand the experience of Native Americans. Both books are illustrated by David J. Catrow, III.

Stevens, Janet. (1993). *Coyote Steals the Blanket: A Ute Tale.* New York: Holiday House. Grades K–2.

Stevens' retelling and superb illustrations of a coyote tale from the native people of present-day Utah make a delightful book for young children. When Coyote takes a blanket he has found in the desert, a large boulder begins chasing him. Coyote solicits the help of several animals to stop the "killer rock," but it's Hummingbird who is able to help him. Children will be amused by this story of a stubborn coyote.

Tanaka, Béatrice. (1991). *The Chase.* New York, Crown Publishers. Grades K–2. (Kutenai)

In a short preface, the author explains that the Kutenai originally lived in present-day Washington, Idaho, and British Columbia. Now most of the 4,000 Kutenai live on their own land in Montana and Idaho. In this simple story, Coyote assumes hunters are coming because he sees

Rabbit running through the forest. Soon other animals also start running. Rabbit finally stops and the animals ask him why they are running. He does not know why all the other animals are running, but he is running because he is late for dinner! With watercolor illustrations, by Michael Gay, this simple story will delight children.

Van Loan, Nancy. (1989). *Rainbow Crow.* New York: Alfred A. Knopf. Grades K–2. (Lenape)

This ancient tale from the Lenape tribe that lived in present-day Pennsylvania tells of the first snowfall on earth and how Crow was once a multicolored bird. The snowfall would not stop. Rainbow Crow decided to go to Great Sky and ask him for help and Crow was given the gift of fire. As Crow came to earth to melt the snow, soot covered his beautiful feathers, and smoke and ashes made his voice cracked and hoarse. Great Sky heard Crow crying and gave him the gift of freedom, promising Crow that the two-legged would never hunt him. The beautiful illustrations by Beatriz Vidal complement the feeling of the story. The magnificent colors of Rainbow Crow help the reader understand the bird's sorrow when his feathers turn black.

Viola, Herman J. (1993). *Osceola.* Austin, TX: Steck-Vaughn Company. Grades 3–5. (Florida Seminole)

White people had difficulty pronouncing the name of Chief *Asi-Yaholo*, instead calling him *Osceola* (AHS cee oh la). Osceola and the Seminole people welcomed runaway slaves into their tribe. This angered white slaveowners, who wanted the Seminoles to return the slaves. When the U.S. government attempted to force the Seminoles to leave Florida and move to Indian Territory, Osceola united his people against the government. Viola tells the compelling story of the member of the Creek tribe who became a great Seminole chief. The color illustrations by Yoshi Miyake show the beauty of the Seminole homeland and depict Osceola as a competent leader. Another book by the same author in the Native American Stories series is *Sitting Bull* (1992), the story of the Lakota (Sioux) chief who defeated Lieutenant Colonel Custer at Little Big Horn.

Yolen, Jane. (1990). *Sky Dogs.* San Diego: Harcourt Brace Jovanovich. Grades K–2. (Blackfeet)

Several tribes tell the story of how the first horse arrived. When the horses appeared, the Blackfeet thought they were large dogs sent to them by the creator, Old Man. This story is the recollection of He-who-loves-horses, an old man, of when the first horses came to his people. Yolen's first-person narrative reads like a folktale being passed on to the next generation. Earth-tone colors are used by Barry Moser to depict life on the American plains. The author's note at the end of the story provides added information about the Blackfeet and the coming of the horse.

CONTEMPORARY SETTINGS

Although many Native American tribes, such as the Hopi of Arizona, maintain a traditional lifestyle similar to that of their ancestors, the majority of native people live in a dual world (Little Soldier 1982). Many have taken on some North American characteristics while maintaining their own culture. The following titles are depictions of Native Americans in contemporary settings who continue to practice their traditions.

Baylor, Byrd. (1976). *Hawk I'm Your Brother*. New York: Charles Scribner's Sons. Grades K–2. (Diné)

Rudy Soto, a young Diné (Navajo), would like to be more like Hawk, whose freedom and ability to fly are what Rudy most desires. Baylor's text and the pencil drawings of Peter Parnall work together to tell a simple story that reflects the culture of the Diné.

Baylor has written several other books that also depict accurately the contemporary life of various native tribes. They include *And It Is Still That Way* (1976), a collection of stories told by Native American children; *The Desert Is Theirs* (1975), about the Tohono O'odham Nation (formally referred to as the Papago tribe) of southern Arizona; *I'm In Charge of Celebrations* (1986), a young Native American girl's descriptions of the beauty of the desert; and *Moonsong* (1982), a Pima Nation (Arizona) tale of how the coyote is a child of the moon.

Coombs, Linda. (1992). *Powwow*. Cleveland, OH: Modern Curriculum Press. Grades K–2. (Wampanoags and Penobscot)

Tina Howowswee and her family, of the Wampanoag tribe in Massachusetts, have been traveling from one powwow to another all summer. This powwow is special for Tina because there she will compete in the dance competition for the first time. Elements of the culture of various tribes from across North America, such as *"Navajo tacos,"* *"buffalo burgers,"* and native arts and crafts, are mentioned in this work. The illustrations by Carson Waterman show details of the *regalia*, traditional native clothing. Coombs, a member of the Wampanoag tribe, has helped organize many powwows, and her familiarity with this special event is evident. A glossary at the end of the book explains some of the words associated with a powwow. This title, from the Multicultural Celebrations series, was created under the auspices of The Children's Museum in Boston. Another Native American title in the series is *Strawberry Thanksgiving* (1992) by Paula Jennings, with illustrations by Ramona Peters.

Davis, Deborah. (1989). *The Secret of the Seal.* New York: Crown Publishers. Grades 6–8. (Inuit)

This book is set in an isolated Inuit village in Alaska. Kyo (pronounced KEY oh), is unable to kill his first seal

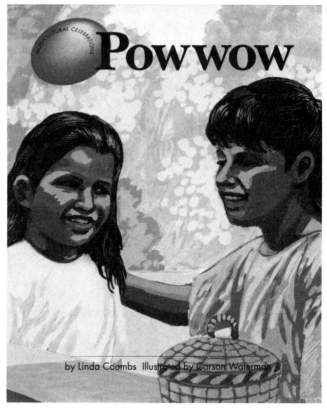

FIGURE 6-4 *Powwow* by Linda Coombs. © 1992 by The Children's Museum, Boston. Cover reprinted by permission of Modern Curriculum Press, Inc.

whom he befriends and names Tookey. When his Uncle George comes to hunt for a seal to be taken to a zoo, Kyo fears that Tookey will be captured. As an Inuit, Kyo begins wrestling with the fact that he is making a pet out of a seal when he should be hunting seals for his family. This story shows some aspects of Inuit culture, such as the hunting of seal and caribou and the making of bread. The author provides a glimpse of how modern conveniences such as the snowmobile have made life easier for the Inuit, just as the horse made life easier for the people of the Great Plains. Although this book does not depict the harsh realities of living in the far north, it does depict something of the Inuit way of life. The black and white illustrations are by Judy Labrasca.

Erdrich, Heidi Ellen. (1993). *Maria Tallchief.* Austin, TX: Steck-Vaughn Company. Grades 3–5. (Osage)

Maria Tallchief, born Betty Marie Tall Chief in Oklahoma, had a great talent for playing musical instruments and dancing. When she was eight years old, her family moved to Los Angeles. There she became a great ballet dancer. She later danced for the Ballet Russe and changed her name to Maria Tallchief. From the Native American Stories series, this is an informative introduction to ballet. Maria Tallchief was one of several Native American women who became professional ballet dancers. The color illustrations by Rick Whipple depict the high and low points of her career. The book will appeal to children of diverse backgrounds who have an interest in the fine arts.

Other books in this series that concern modern Native Americans are Edward F. Rivinus' *Jim Thorpe* (1992), the story of the great athlete from the Sauk and Fox tribes, and Jacki Thompson Rand's *Wilma Mankiller* (1993), the biography of the first woman elected Principal Chief of the Cherokee.

Ferris, Jeri. (1991). *Native American Doctor: The Story of Susan LaFlesche Picotte.* Minneapolis: Carolrhoda Books. Grades 3–5. (Omaha)

Susan LaFlesche was born to Iron Eagle, whose English name was Joseph LaFlesche, and to One Woman, whose English name was Mary Gale. Iron Eagle decided not to give his daughter or her sisters Omaha names. When Susan was born in 1865, the traditional ways of Native Americans were coming to an end. This is the story of an Omaha woman who, at the age of 24, became the first Native American doctor. Dr. LaFlesche returned to the Omaha Reservation to care for her people, and she was also a spokesperson, teacher, counselor, and advisor until her death at the age of 50.

George, Jean Craighead. (1987). *The Talking Earth.* New York: HarperCollins. Grades 6–8. (Florida Seminole)

This book teaches the simple lesson that we must care for the earth's resources if we are to survive. Billie Wind is a 13-year-old Seminole girl who does not believe in little people who live underground or the great serpent who lives in the Everglades.

The story examines the conflicts between the old and the new. Billie Wind follows some of the ancient ways of her people, but she has also attended the Kennedy Space Center School and pollution and nuclear war are much more real to her than serpents and little people. In the Everglades, with the help of an otter, a panther, and a turtle, she begins to learn how the old ways can help solve these contemporary problems.

Hausman, Gerald. (1989). *Turtle Dream: Collected Stories from the Hopi, Navajo, Pueblo, and Havasupai People.* Santa Fe, NM: Mariposa Publishing. Grades 6–8.

In this collection of stories, based on the experiences of the author, the values and lifestyles of the Hopi, Diné, Pueblo, and Havasupai are introduced. In "Havasu Sam," two young Diné men who haven't seen each other for about eight years reminisce about their childhood. They try to find the right words to describe their friendship, and one of them states that there are no words in their native language that mean "I love you." The other points out that there is *ayo anoshni*, meaning "I like you a lot." Other stories describe everyday events from the perspective of one of these groups of native people. Hausman has provided a collection of entertaining and enlightening short stories.

TURTLE DREAM

Collected Stories from the Hopi, Navajo, Pueblo, and Havasupai People

Written by Gerald Hausman
Illustrated by Sid Hausman

FIGURE 6-5 *Turtle Dream: Collected Stories from the Hopi, Navajo, Pueblo, and Havasupai People* by Gerald Hausman. Copyright © 1989 by Mariposa Publishing. Cover reprinted by permission of Mariposa Publishing.

Hirschfelder, Arlene. (1986). *Happily May I Walk: American Indians and Alaska Natives Today.* New York: Charles Scribner's Sons. Grades 6–8. (Various tribes)

The dance, music, politics, art, education, religion, language, and other aspects of the culture of the various American Indian and Alaska native tribes are introduced to young readers in this book. The information provided is contemporary and also focuses on current Native American issues such as economics and education. The two-page map at the end of the book shows where Native American tribes are located in the continental United States and Alaska.

Hoyt-Goldsmith, Diane. (1993). *Cherokee Summer.* New York: Holiday House. Grades 3–5. (Cherokee)

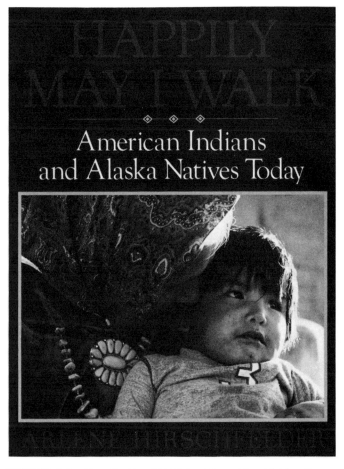

FIGURE 6-6 *Happily May I Walk* by Alene Hirschfelder. Copyright © 1989 by the author. Cover reprinted by permission of John C. Goodwin/United Methodist Church.

With the help of color photographs, illustrations, and maps, the history and contemporary life of the Cherokee are described through the eyes of Bridget, a 10-year-old girl. The Trail of Tears, Cherokee self-government, contemporary family life, and Cherokee traditions and language are all explained. A Cherokee legend is also told. This is an excellent book with which to begin a study of the Cherokee or of Native Americans. The faces of various Native Americans shown on page 27 provide nonstereotyped images of Native Americans.

Miles, Miska. (1971). *Annie and the Old One.* Boston: Little, Brown and Company. Grades 3–5. (Diné)

Annie's grandmother, the Old One, prepares for her impending death by weaving a rug on a loom. Annie has a difficult time dealing with the news, and begins to distract her grandmother from completing the rug. Only after the Old One discusses the cycle of life with Annie does she finally accept her grandmother's death. With simple pencil drawings by Peter Parnall, Miles emphasizes the beauty of the Diné (Navajo) culture in this story written over two decades ago. Aspects of modern life are interwoven with the ancient ways to reflect the contemporary culture of the Diné. For example, Annie goes to and from school in a yellow bus, but her father continues the tradition of working with silver. The story and its universal theme will appeal to both children and adults.

Peters, Russell M. (1992). *Clambake: A Wampanoag Tradition.* Minneapolis, MN: Lerner Publications. Grades K–2. (Wampanoag)

This depiction of the contemporary life of the Wampanoag people is the story of a grandfather teaching his grandson the Wampanoag tradition of the *Appanaug* (meaning seafood cooking or clambake). A ceremony celebrating the changing of the seasons or honoring an important person in the tribe, the clambake involves special ceremonial tasks. Written by a member of the Wampanoag tribe, this book, with its maps and color photographs, does an excellent job of depicting a contemporary Native American home and culture. Another book from Lerner Publications that explains a traditional Native American custom is Gordon Regguinti's *The Sacred Harvest: Ojibway Wild Rice Gathering* (1992).

Swentzell, Rina. (1992). *Children of Clay: A Family of Pueblo Potters.* Minneapolis, MN: Lerner Publications. Grades K–2. (Pueblo)

Written by a member of the Santa Clara Pueblo Tribe, this story concerns a contemporary Pueblo Indian family. With photographs by Bill Steen, it introduces the reader to *Gia* (Tewa word meaning mother) Rose and her large extended family. As Gia Rose and her family trek to the mountains for clay, the collective history of the Pueblo Indians and the Spanish is discussed along with Pueblo folklore. Several maps support the text of this entertaining book.

REFERENCES

Byler, M. G. (1977). American Indian authors for young readers. In MacCann, D. and G. Woodard, ed., *Cultural Conformity in Books for Children.* Metuchen, NJ: Scarecrow Press.

Bulla, C. R. and M. Syson, (1978). *Conquista!* New York: Crowell.

Cullinan, B. E. (1989). *Literature and the Child,* 2nd ed. New York: Harcourt Brace Jovanovich.

Esbensen, B. J. (1988). *The Star Maiden.* Boston: Little, Brown and Company.

Goley, E. (1992). United States: Native Americans. In Miller-Lachmann, L., ed., *Our Family, Our Friends, Our World: An Annotated Guide to Significant Multicultural Books for Children and Teenagers.* New York: R. R. Bowker.

Hirschfelder, Arlene. (1986). *Happily may I walk: American Indians and Alaska Natives today.* New York: Charles Scribner's Sons.

Highwater, J. (1977). *Anpao: An American Indian odessey.* New York: HarperCollins.

LaFromboise, T. D. and K. G. Low, (1989). American Indian Children and Adolescents. In Gibbs, J. T., L. N. Huang and Associates, ed., *Children of color.* San Francisco: Jossey-Bass.

Little Soldier, L. (1982). Now's the time to dispel the myths about Indians. *Learning Magazine, 7,* 44-47.

Little Soldier, L. (1992). Working With Native American Children. *Young Children, 47,* 15-21.

Norton, D. E. (1991). *Through the eyes of a child: An introduction to children's literature,* 3rd ed. New York: Macmillan.

7 ACTIVITIES FOR EXTENDING CHILDREN'S EXPERIENCES WITH MULTIETHNIC LITERATURE

When children read multiethnic children's literature, they learn that others have experienced joys, fears, and disappointments similar to their own. Hopefully, this instills in children a lifelong love of reading and an appreciation for the ideas contained in the literature, even when the context is different from their own culture. As children learn to appreciate literature, they also gain strength in problem solving (Rothlein & Meinbach, 1991). The activities suggested in this chapter will give educators ideas for extending children's experience with literature. Whether it is by helping children feel good about their own culture or by developing their understanding of other cultures, these activities can be of value to all children. Some of them can be easily adapted to different books while others deal with a specific culture.

LATINO CHILDREN'S LITERATURE

Winter, J. and Winter, J. (1991). *Diego.* New York: Alfred A. Knopf.

Activity #1: Create a circular story map. On your story map, sketch the experiences of Diego.

Example:

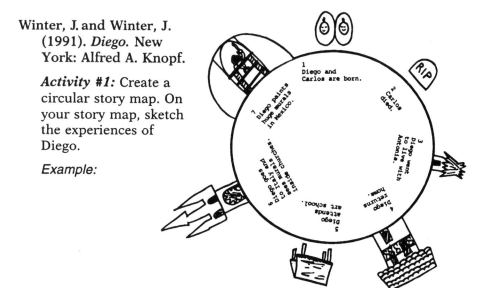

Activity #2: Write the following questions on cards in the shape of Antonia's house. Children will use higher-level thinking skills to answer the questions.

Questions:

- When Diego became ill, where was he taken? (Antonia, an Indian healer, took him to her hut in the mountains.)
- When Diego began painting, what did he want to paint? (He wanted to paint scenes from real life.)
- How would this story have been different if Diego had not gone to Italy?
- Would you like to be Diego's friend? Why or why not?
- If you were to paint scenes from your real life, what would you paint?
- Compare Diego's life as a child to your life. How is it like yours? How is it different?
- Murals have been painted on buildings, walls, and ceilings. Think of a new place to paint a mural. What would you paint there? Why?

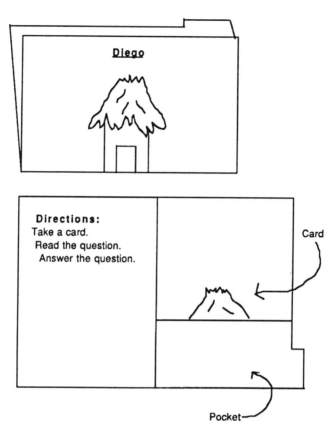

Zapater, B. (1992). *Fiesta!* Cleveland, OH: Modern Curriculum Press.

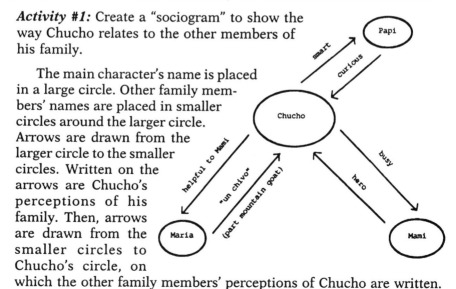

Activity #1: Create a "sociogram" to show the way Chucho relates to the other members of his family.

The main character's name is placed in a large circle. Other family members' names are placed in smaller circles around the larger circle. Arrows are drawn from the larger circle to the smaller circles. Written on the arrows are Chucho's perceptions of his family. Then, arrows are drawn from the smaller circles to Chucho's circle, on which the other family members' perceptions of Chucho are written.

Activity #2: A different type of sociogram shows the relationships between characters.

Example:

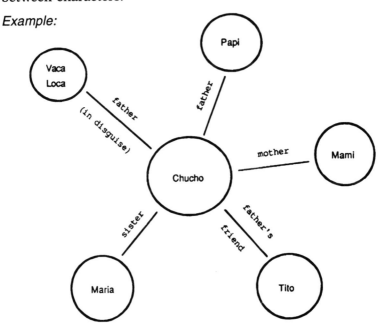

Activity #3: Create an *acrostic* describing the fiesta.

Example:

Food

Inspiration

Exciting

Shouting

Trajes Típicos

Anticipation

Activity #4: Design your own mask for a fiesta. Name it. Use details to show how it received its name. You need to decide what materials to use for your mask. Some masks are made from common items like paper plates, construction paper, or cardboard boxes. You may want to use paper maché to construct your mask. When the paper maché is dry, it can be painted. Use your creativity and imagination when adding details to your mask. Yarn, string, rocks, glitter, felt, and many other items can be used.

Something to think about:

- What does *Vaca Loca* mean?

- Look at the picture of *Vaca Loca* in the book. What makes it look like a wild cow?

Activity #5: Create a folder for this story, containing question cards with the following questions.

- What is a *palo encebao*? (a greased pole)

- What did Chucho do that made him the hero of the day? (Chucho climbed up on Papi's shoulders and reached the prize.)

- Think of another way to reach the prize on top of the *palo encebao*.

- How did Mami's feelings change about *un chivo* during the story? Give examples.

- Have you ever felt like a hero? What did you do to become a hero? How did you feel?

- Compare the fiesta described in this book with a celebration in your town (for example, the Fourth of July).

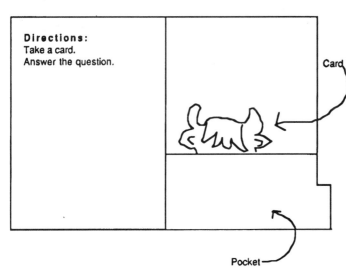

Rohmer, M. (1982). *The Legend of Food Mountain.*
La montaña del alimento. San Francisco:
Children's Book Press.

Activity #1: Create a "wanted" poster for the
rain dwarfs. Include their crimes and a possible
reward.

Example:

Activity #2: Write a *cinquain* describing a character in the story.

The cinquain is a five-line poem written in the following format:

Line 1: One word (may be the title)
Line 2: Two words (describing the title)
Line 3: Three words (actions)
Line 4: Four words (feeling)
Line 5: One word (referring to title)

Example:

Villains

Bold, Greedy

Stealing, Taking, Eating

Shock, Sadness, Hunger, Anger

Dwarfs

Activity #3: Write a *diamante* contrasting Quetzalcoatl and the Rain Dwarfs.

A diamante is a poem written in the following format:

Line 1: One word (noun or pronoun)
Line 2: Two words (adjectives describing line 1)
Line 3: Three words ("ing" verbs describing actions related to line 1)
Line 4: Four words (nouns: first two relate to line 1, last two to line 7)
Line 5: Three words ("ing" verbs describing actions related to line 7)
Line 6: Two words (adjectives describing line 7)
Line 7: One word (noun or pronoun, often the opposite of the word in line 1)

Example:

Quetzalcoatl

Great, Powerful

Creating, Searching, Feeding

Magic, Caring, Selfish, Ruthless

Stealing, Taking, Eating

Bold, Greedy

Dwarfs

Activity #4: Analyze one of the characters in this story.

Write the character's name in a large circle in the middle of the page. Write the qualities of the character in smaller circles. Draw lines connecting the smaller circles to the center circle. On the lines write examples of an action, conversation, or comment that helped reflect that quality.

powerful

He created the people of the earth.

overjoyed

"Food mountain will feed the people of earth forever."

Quatzalcoatl

He changed himself into an ant.

magic

McLerran, A. (1992). *I Want to Go Home.* New York: Tambourine Books.

Activity #1: Write a letter from Marta to a friend at the beginning of the story. Now write a letter from Marta to a friend at the end of the story. How are the letters different? Why?

Activity #2: Create a lost or found advertisement about Sammy.

Activity #3: Make a set of cat cards. On each card write a question about the story. Store in a folder.

Questions:

• Why was Marta sad? (She had moved to a new home.)

• What made Marta realize that her new home was "home?"

LOST!

SAMMY, THE CAT

(When she was comforting Sammy and telling him, "Everything's going to be okay. This is home now," she realized it was her home now, too.)

- Have you ever had a special pet that helped you when you were lonely? Tell about it.
- What other way could Marta feel at home in her new house?
- How might the story have been different if Sammy had run away?
- Predict what will happen to Marta and Sammy in the future.

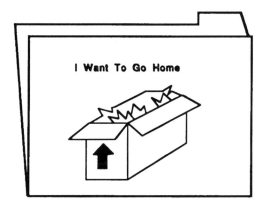

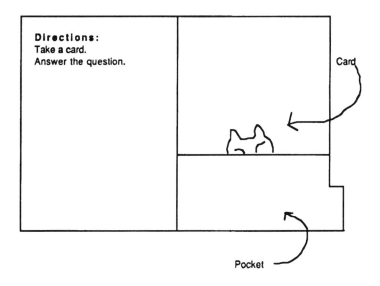

Aardema, V. (1991). *Borreguita and the Coyote.* New York: Alfred A. Knopf.

Activity #1: Make Borreguita cards with questions from the story.

Questions:

- What was Borreguita doing when she met Coyote?

- Why did Coyote agree to wait to eat Borreguita?

- What happens to you when you play tricks on people? Has a trick you've played ever gotten anyone in trouble?

- Compare the Borreguita and the Coyote. How are they alike? How are they different?

- Think of a new way the Borreguita could trick Coyote.

- Will the Coyote have anything to eat now that he has decided not to eat the Borreguita? Explain your answer.

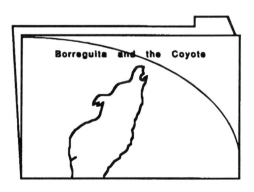

Borreguita and the Coyote

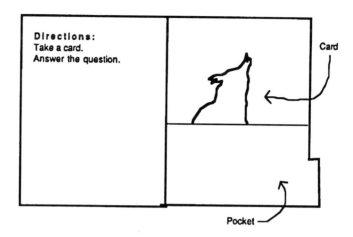

Activity #2: Record the different ways the Borreguita tricked the Coyote on the circular story map.

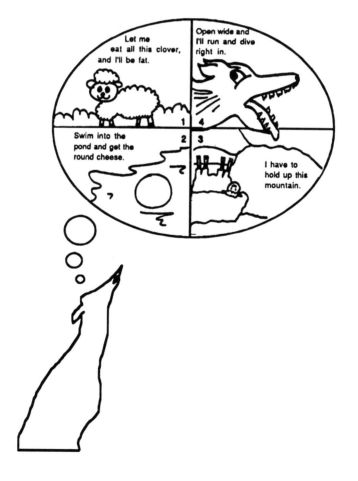

Activity #3: Make a "wanted" poster describing food for Coyote.

Example:

Wanted!

Borreguita with these qualifications:

- already fat;
- afraid of water;
- too weak to hold up a mountain; and
- not a fast runner.

Interested borreguitas need to apply in person:

Coyote's Corner
1111 Flat Dry Plain

Activity #4: Record the events of the story from the Coyote's point of view in a diary.

Example:

Day One

Dear Diary,

   I met a scrumptuous-looking Borreguita today. I could have eaten her, but being the cunning coyote that I am, I am planning to eat her when she has "fattened up" on the clover. You should have seen how much she was eating! My mouth is already watering just thinking about it!

AFRICAN AMERICAN CHILDREN'S LITERATURE

Havill, J. (1989). *Jamaica Tag-Along.* Boston: Houghton Mifflin Company.

Activity #1: Put the following questions on basketball-shaped cards. Store in a folder labeled "Jamaica Tag-Along."

- Why did Jamaica want to shoot baskets with Ossie and Buzz? (She didn't have anything to do.)

- Describe how Jamaica feels when Ozzie tells her not to tag along.

- If you didn't have anyone to play with, what are some things you could do by yourself?

- Compare Jamaica's relationship with Ossie and her relationship with Berto. How are the two relationships alike? How are they different?

- How would the story have ended if Ossie had allowed Jamaica to shoot baskets with him?

- Have you ever been told not to tag along? How did it make you feel?

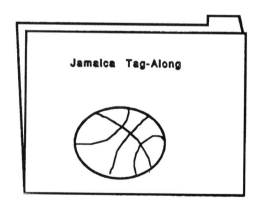

Jamaica Tag-Along

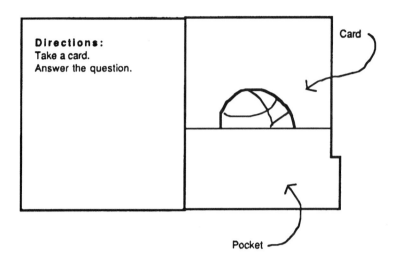

Activity #2: Record the events of the story in a diary from Ossie's point of view.

Example:

> Dear Diary,
>
>   What a great day to shoot baskets? Well it would have been, except for Jamaica! She always bothers me when I want to play with my friends! I always have to babysit her until Mom comes home from work, so when I get to play with friends, I don't want her around! Maybe tomorrow she will have friends of her own to play with.

Activity #3: Choose one of the following ideas for a letter.

• Write a letter to Jamaica describing a time when your feelings were hurt. Tell her how you handled the hurt feelings.

• Pretend you are Ossie. Write a letter to Jamaica. Explain why you don't want her around when you play with your friends.

Lowery, L. (1987). *Martin Luther King Day*. New York: Scholastic.

Activity #1: Organize an African American History Fair to be held on Martin Luther King Day or to culminate Black History Month (February).

Suggestions:

- Each classroom will select an African American to study.
- The teacher and students will research this person and prepare a display to be entered in the History Fair.
- Displays should be set up the day before the actual History Fair.
- Judges from the community will judge the displays and award prizes.
- Publicize! Invite the community to visit the African American History Fair. Have a program printed to guide visitors through the various projects.

Activity #2: Write a bio-poem about Dr. Martin Luther King.

A bio-poem tells about a famous person, real or fictitious, using the following format:

Line 1: First Name
Line 2: Title
Line 3: Four words (that describe the person)
Line 4: Lover of (three or more things or ideas)
Line 5: Who believed (one or more ideas)
Line 6: Who wanted (three things)
Line 7: Who used (three things or methods)
Line 8: Who gave (three things)
Line 9: Who said (a quote)
Line 10: Last name

Example:

Martin Luther

Minister

Just, Courageous, Eloquent, Fair

Lover of Freedom, Justice, and Equality

Who believed the world could be a better place

Who wanted Peace, Respect, and Hope

Who used Preaching, Nonviolence, and Love

Who gave Help, Time, and His Life

Who said "let freedom ring"

King

Medearis, A. (1992). *The Zebra-Riding Cowboy*. New York: Henry Holt & Company.

Activity #1: Retell the story so that it takes place today. How will it change? Create a diorama contrasting the story as written and as retold in modern times. (Suggestion: Divide the diorama into two sections or create two dioramas.)

Activity #2: Imagine you are the horse Zebra Dun. Rewrite the story from the horse's point of view. Make it into a play. Act out the story with some other students.

Activity #3: In your library, find information on African American cowboys such as Bose Ikard, One-Horse Charlie, Bill Pickett, and

Nat "Dead-Eye Dick" Love. Make a chart showing similarities and differences among the people you read about.

Example:

Name	Similarities	Differences
Bose Ikard		
Bill Pickett		

Activity #4: Meet the author.

Write a letter to the author. Tell the author what you found interesting about the book. Write about how you could relate to a character or situation in the book. Interview the author by mail. Ask thought-provoking questions of the writer. Authors' addresses can be found in books such as *Major Authors and Illustrators for Children and Young Adults.* Publishing Info: Nakamura, Joyce and Collier, Laurie. *Major Authors and Illustrators for Children and Young Adults.* Detroit: Gale Research, 1992.

This was the author's response when asked what suggestions she had to help educators help children become writers.

> I think that a book production center in a classroom is one of the best ways to increase a student's writing skills. I've received dozens of letters from students who have written and published their own books. My favorite letter is from a little girl in the first grade: 'I've written 16 books! How many have you written?' The books she had written were in the same format as a commercially published book, down to a photograph/bio of the author on the last page. If she's this excited about writing at age 6, I'd venture to say that she'll retain that excitement at age 60.
>
> The children have the same pride and joy when seeing their work in a book form that I do when I receive my new books from the publisher. The children's artwork and stories are wonderful and the sheer pleasure and the sense of accomplishment they gain from writing lasts a lifetime.

Establishing a book production center is inexpensive and also a wonderful way to teach children every stage of book production from expressing an idea to the finished product. Children work in groups and develop editing and communication skills in writing that are overlooked in typical writing assignments. I'm looking forward to the generation of published authors to come. After all, most of them had 16 books written by the time they were six!

On the value of African American Children's literature for African American and non-African American children:

I love the new emphasis on multicultural literature. I don't remember ever reading a picture book with an African American character in it as a child. I can't describe the joy of finding a book that strikes close to home and seeing a reflection of people who look just like you between the covers. I also think that it is just as important for non-African American children to find that their feelings and situations mirror those of a nonwhite child. The lesson is that we have more in common than we think we do.

I think that some publishers feel that the key to all this is just having more minority characters. Those who feel that way are still missing the boat to the new world. Soon minorities will be the majority. We don't want caricatures of our culture, we want reality.

This is not to say that minorities don't have a wide range of experiences. I know that some experiences are common to all of us, regardless of race. My point is that your background and your culture are going to be the framework in which you relate to that experience.

If I wrote a book about my first day at school, the fear of having my mother leave me would probably strike a common chord with many of my readers. However, my observation that I was the only African-American child in the entire class, and the things that happened as a result of that, would not be. When I read books that have a general storyline, I can relate to the common human experience. However, if the characters are African American I expect to find the cultural link I share with that character.

Exploring how our cultural background influences us within the framework of a story is an important method of helping us to understand one another. I think that there will always be racial hatred and prejudice as long as we fear the things we perceive as 'different' about a person. Exploring our differences and our similarities is an important part of bridging the gap between races.

(Interview, January, 1993)

Other books by this author include *Picking Peas for a Penny, Dancing With the Indians, Rum-A-Tum-Tum, From Africa to America, Treemonisha, Poppa's New Pants, The Christmas Riddle, Littls Louis and the Jazz Band,* and *Sing, Coretta Sing.*

Ringgold, R. (1991). *Tar Beach.* New York: Crown Publishers, Inc.

Activity #1: In this story, Cassie Louise dreams that she claims the buildings as her own as she "flies" over the city. As she says, "All you need is somewhere to go that you can't get to any other way. The next thing you know, you're flying among the stars."

Have you ever had a dream to go somewhere or be someone you've never been? What is your dream? How would you choose to illustrate your dream? Create an illustration of your dream.

If you have never had a dream to go somewhere or be someone you've never been, imagine where you would go if you could go anywhere. Imagine who you would be if you could be anyone. Write about your new destination or new identity. Illustrate these imaginings.

Activity #2: The author of this story used a quilt to illustrate her dream. Her slave ancestors made quilts as part of their plantation duties. Do research to find out about the quilting done by slaves. Also find out about quilting done by other groups. How are the different types of quilting similar? How are they different? Design a quilt depicting some aspect of your life.

You may want to use paper to design your quilt. You and your classmates could put your ideas together and design a classroom quilt, with each student designing one square. The squares would depict the special talents of each student. Draw the designs on squares of fabric (10" × 10" is a good size). Using fabric paints, color the designs. Ask an adult, maybe your teacher, to sew the fabric squares together. Display the quilt in a hallway in your school.

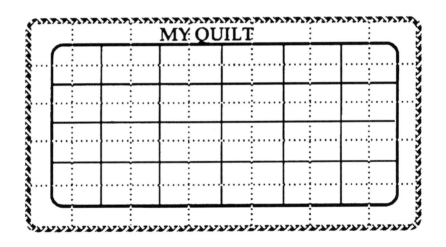

Tate, E. (1990). *Thank You, Dr. Martin Luther King, Jr.!* New York: Bantam Skylark Book.

Activity #1: In this story, Mary Elouise was ashamed of her heritage until some storytellers came to her classroom and told some African tales. One of the stories they told was "Why Mosquitoes Buzz in People's Ears."

Find a copy of "Why Mosquitoes Buzz in People's Ears." Read it and prepare to tell the story to your class.

Activity #2: How would this story be different if Brandy had wanted Mary Elouise for a friend? Would Mary Elouise have become proud of her African roots? Write the new ending.

Activity #3: Have you ever wished you were different and looked like someone else? Why or why not? Write about those feelings.

ASIAN AMERICAN CHILDREN'S LITERATURE

Yen, C. (1991). *Why Rat Comes First.* San Francisco: Children's Book Press.

> *Activity #1:* In this story, the Jade King proclaimed Rat the winner. He also said that all children born in the year of the Rat would be as clever as Rat.
>
> • How did Rat make the children choose him?
>
> • Think of five other clever ways Rat could have made the children choose him.
>
> • Think of five clever ways Ox could have been the children's choice.
>
> • Think of one new clever idea and rewrite the ending of the story.
>
> *Activity #2:* In the back of this book, the 12 animals are listed.
>
> Look at the characteristics of Rat and at those of Dragon, Monkey, and Horse. Why do you think that Rat will get along with Dragon and Monkey? Why will he *not* get along with Horse?
>
> Look at the characteristics of Rat and Ox. Why do you suppose Rat was able to think of a way to win the personality contest? How could Ox use his characteristics to recapture the children's votes?
>
> Rat and Ox each wanted the first year named for him. Think of the other animals. Which animal would you choose to be the first? Why?

Tompert, A. (1990). *Grandfather Tang's Story.* New York: Crown Publishers.

> *Activity #1:* Make your own *tangram* (trace and cut out).

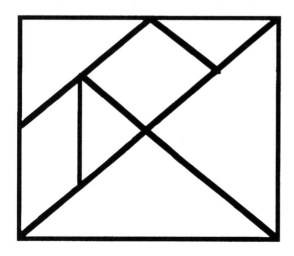

A tangram begins with a square. It is cut into 7 standard pieces. Each piece is called a *tan.* To make a picture, all 7 tans must touch, but not overlap.

- Recreate the pictures from the story. Create three new pictures with your tans.

- Write a story using your three new pictures.

Activity #2: In this story, the hunter shot Chou's wing and tried to catch him. Wu Ling then changed into a lion to protect his friend.

- Choose a different animal for Wu Ling to become. Write a new ending. Use your tangram to create the animal you choose.

Activity #3: Little Soo was listening to Grandfather Tang "tell the story." Grandparents can be excellent storytellers. Name five other activities grandchildren enjoy with their grandparents. Which do you like most? Why?

Activity #4: Grandfather Tang used a tangram to illustrate his story as he was telling it. Think of some other ways to illustrate a story. Choose one and use it to illustrate the story of Chou and Wu Ling.

Ziong, B. (1989). *Nine-In-One Grr! Grr!* San Francisco: Children's Book Press.

Activity #1: Tiger had to make up a song to sing to help her remember the important words.

- Think of songs you know that help you remember something. Name them.

- Think of something you are learning in school right now. Make up your own song to help you remember the important points. (You may want to use a song you already know, changing the words to make a new song.)

- Memorize the song.

- Share it with the rest of your class.

Activity #2: How would the story have been different if Bird had gone to ask the great Shao how many babies she would have?

- What would Bird's song have been?

- How would Tiger have tricked Bird into forgetting her song?

- Why would Tiger want Bird to forget the words?

Activity #3: As Tiger traveled to see the great Shao, how was the landscape described?

- Think of the landscape where you live. If Tiger made the journey through your land, how might it be described?

- Illustrate your landscape.

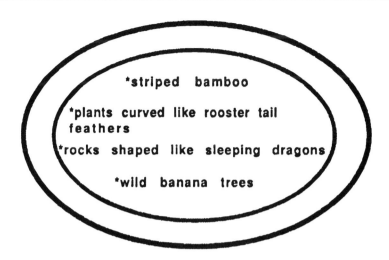

*striped bamboo

*plants curved like rooster tail feathers

*rocks shaped like sleeping dragons

*wild banana trees

Sing, R. (1992). *Chinese New Year's Dragon.* Cleveland, OH: Modern Curriculum Press.

Activity #1: Using the chart, find the date for this year's Chinese New Year. Mark it on your calendar and make plans to recognize the Chinese New Year in your classroom.

Chinese New Year
Friday, February 11, 1994
Tuesday, January 31, 1995
Friday, January 19, 1996
Friday, February 7, 1997
Wednesday, January 28, 1998
Monday, February 15, 1999
Friday, February 4, 2000

Once you have marked the appropriate date, organize a Dragon Contest. (This can be done in one classroom or schoolwide.)

Each student, group, or class will design and create their own dragon for Chinese New Year. Some suggestions might include:

Dragon Kite
Dragon Piñata
Dragon-decorated T-Shirt
Dragon Costume

Ask people from the community to judge the dragons. Announce the winners at your Chinese New Year's celebration.

Activity #2: The family in this story practiced many traditions in celebration of Chinese New Year.

Name some of these traditions.

Examples:

• Decorating with flowers

• Eating roasted seeds and dried fruits

• Making and eating *jiaozi* to remind people about friendship and family togetherness

• Serving long noodles to symbolize long life

• Giving *hongbao*, which means red envelope, with "lucky money" inside

Compare and contrast these traditions with the traditions your family follows on New Year's Eve and Day.

Yep, L. (1991). *The Star Fisher.* New York: Morrow Junior Books.

Activity #1: The Star Fisher takes place in 1927. If you wanted to learn more about life in this country in the 1920s, what items from that decade might help you?

Sometimes people use a *time capsule* to preserve information about the present for the future. Instructions are usually left regarding when and by whom the time capsule may be opened. Imagine that you have been assigned to design and construct a time capsule that will show children in the future the kinds of books you enjoy reading today.

• What items from *The Star Fisher*, might you use to represent the story?

• In what shape might your time capsule be?

Make your time capsule and include important items from this story.

Example:

> Make the time capsule in the shape of a star. Cut the shape out of a paper bag, fill it with the items from the story, and staple the sides together. Remember to include the title of the story on the outside of the time capsule. It might include a letter from Joan Lee to a friend back in Ohio telling of her new life in West Virginia, a recipe for apple pie, and a copy of the story of the star fishers.

Activity #2: This story takes place in 1927. In it Joan Lee compares her life with that of a star fisher. Is the story of the star fishers relevant today? Apply it to your life or to the life of someone you know. Write about how your life is similar to that of the star fisher. How is your life different?

Activity #3: Every school receives new students throughout the school year. In *The Star Fisher*, Joan Lee does not feel welcome at her new school. Think of the new students who come to your school. Do they feel welcome? If so, what happens at your school to make them feel welcome? If not, what do you think would make new students feel welcome at your school? One idea for welcoming new students is to create a brochure including important information for new students. Plan, design, and create such a brochure for new students. What kind of information should a new student know about your school? Where can a new student go for help in your school? Are there any organizations in your school that help make new students feel welcome? Include everything that will make this New Student Orientation Brochure truly helpful to new students. Present your finished brochure to your teacher or principal. Ask if it would be possible to print some brochures for future new students.

NATIVE AMERICAN CHILDREN'S LITERATURE

Coombs, L. (1992). *Powwow.* Cleveland, OH: Modern Curriculum Press.

Activity #1: Imagine you are visiting a powwow for the first time. Think about what you hear, smell, and see. Retell this story from your point of view.

Activity #2: In this story, Tina was able to see her friend Joanie only in the summer when their families traveled to powwows.

Imagine it is winter. Tina is with her family in Massachusetts, and Joanie is in Maine. What might Tina tell Joanie about her life in Massachusetts? Write a letter from Tina to Joanie.

Activity #3: Create a diorama of a Powwow. Remember to include composites, food stands, craft booths, and dancing area.

Activity #4: In this story, Tina is going to compete in the Fancy Shawl Dance for the first time ever. How do you think she feels? Have you ever competed in a contest? How did you feel the first time? Write a letter to Tina telling her about your first competition and how you felt.

Ortiz, S. (1988). *The People Shall Continue.* San Francisco: Children's Book Press.

Activity #1: This book tells the history of Native Americans from their beginnings to modern times.

Research your own ethnic group's history. Have your people ever been oppressed? How? Have you ever felt oppressed? How? What traditions does your group pass on to future generations?

Activity #2: In this story, different emotions are expressed. Identify the different emotions found in the story. Think about how each emotion makes people feel. Make masks illustrating each emotion.

Prepare to retell the story to your class in your own words, using the masks at appropriate times.

Ebensen, B. (1989). *Ladder to the Sky.* Boston: Little, Brown and Company.

Activity #1: Retell this story with musical accompaniment. Choose music that best reflects the mood of the story. Will you need different types of music? Is some of the story peaceful and other parts sad? Are there moments when you seem to be holding your breath? How can you use music to convey these changes in feeling?

Record the musical accompaniment and use it to retell the story.

Activity #2: After the vine broke, bringing death and disease, the people were told that plants could be used to cure disease.

Using encyclopedias and other reference books, find out about some plants that have been used to cure sickness and ease pain. Can you think of modern products that have plants as ingredients? Invent a new health product that has one of the plants you learned about in your research as an ingredient. Design an advertisement to promote your product. (Remember to tell about the plant's powers!)

Tanaka, B. (1991). *The Chase*. New York: Crown Publishers.

Activity #1: This story teaches us that we should investigate a situation before we follow along.

Imagine how Bear, Wolf, Moose, and Coyote must have felt when they learned the true reason why they were running. Draw a picture to illustrate how they felt. Make sure the animals' faces show how they felt.

Activity #2: Think of a different reason for why Rabbit was running. How would it change the story ending? Write the new ending.

Activity #3: Imagine you are a news reporter on the scene as Rabbit runs by. You begin to report on Rabbit's amazing speed when all of a sudden Coyote races by after him. You then witness Moose, Wolf, and Bear galloping by at high speed. Write your report for the 6:00 news.

Ata, T. (1989). *Baby Rattlesnake*. San Francisco: Children's Book Press.

Activity #1: In this story, Baby Rattlesnake learns what happens when you get something before you are ready for it.

Think of a different animal that could be used to teach the same lesson. What would this animal get too early that might cause problems? Retell the story from this animal's perspective.

Identify one thing you want, but are too young to get. Retell the story using you and the thing you want to teach the lesson.

Activity #2: Suppose the chief's daughter screamed and ran away instead of smashing Baby Rattlesnake's rattle. How would the story end? Would Baby Rattlesnake learn a lesson about life? Write the new ending to the story.

Illustrate the new ending.

REFERENCES

Rothlein, L. and Meinback, A. (1991). *The Literature Connection, Using Children's Books in the Classroom*. Glenview, IL: Scott, Foresman and Company.

Nakamura, Joyce and Collier, Laurie. (1992). *Major authors and illustrators for children and young adults*. Detroit: Gale Research.

CONCLUSIONS

AMERICA'S RACIAL AND ETHNIC DIVERSITY

In many of our urban schools, African Americans, Latinos, Asian Americans, and Native Americans constitute the majority. Examining current demographic trends, experts have concluded that the children of the four major nonwhite populations will represent four out of ten children in our public schools by the year 2000 (Miller-Lachmann, 1992). Since the United States is a multiethnic nation, we must acknowledge our diversity as a strength rather than a liability.

THE GROWING NEED FOR MULTIETHNIC CHILDREN'S LITERATURE

Although many Americans may not be aware of it, or refuse to acknowledge it, we are what we are as a nation because of the unique contributions that every racial and ethnic group has made to our way of life. Children's literature that reflects the contributions, life styles, and values of these groups will not only help children of color to better understand who they are, it will also teach white majority children to respect the contributions and life styles of individuals who belong to these groups. This is vital if we are to make a smooth transition from a predominately white population to one that is nonwhite in a few more decades.

An important aspect of this transition is the empowerment of our children of color. Because culture plays such an important role in the evolution of a child's sense of self, multiethnic children's books will benefit children of color by allowing them to see themselves in literature. Teachers and other adults who work with children will benefit by becoming familiar with the cultural backgrounds of their students.

The number of excellent books reflecting the culture, heritage, and contemporary experiences of America's people of color continues to be small. Nevertheless, we as educators and caretakers should take every opportunity to use these books so that children have a chance to examine and respond to cultural experiences, values, and beliefs different from their own. We have attempted to provide as many titles as possible to help accomplish that goal.

These books were those we deemed exceptional in accurately depicting the culture of America's people of color and/or in providing good role models for our children and young adults. They will instill in our children a sense of the value of diversity that is essential to our survival as a multiethnic and multicultural society.

IMPLICATIONS FOR THE FUTURE

Children's literature has been enriched by books for and about African Americans, Latinos, Asian Americans, and Native Americans. Authors who write books that focus on multiethnic heritages are providing a valuable service to our children, who someday will be the leaders of our changing society. We must address the lack of multiethnic children's literature if we believe that children must be given the opportunity to learn about the culture and history of North America's culturally different people.

Increasing the number of books reflecting our cultural diversity is essential. Several presses, such as Carolrhoda, Holiday House, and Raintree, have recently addressed this issue by publishing multiethnic titles. A major obstacle that must be overcome is publisher's reluctance to allow authors from the four nonwhite groups to refine their writing skills with each new book. We have seen how Nicholasa Mohr, the renowned Puerto Rican writer, matured with each new story. Other authors outside of mainstream America deserve the same opportunity to grow and mature with each manuscript, rather than merely being offered "one-time shots."

Our federal and state governments must also become involved by providing financial support to authors who speak to our children of color. Federal, state, and local educational agencies must encourage publishers to provide books that show the cultural diversity within our schools.

Finally, small publishing companies committed to producing multiethnic children's literature must be supported and given an opportunity to sell their books to our schools and public libraries. The future seems promising for all our children as we begin to acknowledge our diversity and as we prepare them to take responsibility for the care of our world and its inhabitants. Literature that reflects the experiences of the people of color within our borders is a vital part of that preparation.

REFERENCES

Miller-Lachman, L. (ed.). (1992). *Our Family, Our Friends, Our World: An Annotated Guide to Significant Multicultural Books for Children and Teenagers*. New York: R.R. Bowker.

APPENDIX

PUBLISHERS AND ADDRESSES

ARTE PUBLICO PRESS
University of Houston
Houston, TX 77204-2090

ATHENEUM
866 Third Avenue
New York, NY 10022

BANTAM DOUBLEDAY DELL PUBLISHING
666 Fifth Avenue
New York, NY 10103

PETER BEDRICK BOOKS
2112 Broadway
New York, NY 10023

BILINGUAL EDUCATION SERVICES
1607 Hope Street
South Pasadena, CA 91030

BRADBURY PRESS
866 Third Avenue
New York, NY 10022

CAROLRHODA BOOKS, INC.
241 First Avenue North
Minneapolis, MN 55401

CHILDREN'S BOOK PRESS
1461 Ninth Avenue
San Francisco, CA 94122

CHILDREN'S PRESS
5440 N. Cumberland Avenue
Chicago, IL 60656

CINCO PUNTOS PRESS
2709 Louisville
El Paso, TX 79930

CLARION BOOKS
215 Park Avenue South
New York, NY 10003

CROWN PUBLISHERS, INC.
225 Park Avenue South
New York, NY 10003

DUTTON
375 Hudson Street
New York, NY 10014

EAKIN PRESS
P.O. Drawer 90159
Austin, TX 78709

EDICIONES LIBRERO
Betances Este 166
Mayagüez, Puerto Rico 00708

FRANKLIN WATTS
95 Madison Avenue
New York, NY 10016

FULCRUM PUBLISHING
350 Indiana Street, Suite 350
Golden CO 80401

GARETH STEVENS CHILDREN'S BOOKS
1555 North RiverCenter Drive, Suite 201
Milwaukee, WI 53212

GREENWILLOW BOOKS
105 Madison Avenue
New York, NY 10016

HARCOURT BRACE JOVANOVICH, INC.
6277 Sea Harbor Drive
Orlando, FL 32887

HARPER & ROW, INC.
10 E. 53rd Street
New York, NY 10022

HARPERCOLLINS
300 Reisterstown Road
Baltimore, MD 21208

HOLIDAY HOUSE, INC.
425 Madison Avenue
New York, NY 10017

HENRY HOLT & COMPANY
115 W. 18th Street
New York, NY 10011

HOUGHTON MIFFLIN COMPANY
One Beacon Street
Boston, MA 02108

ALFRED A. KNOPF, INC.
201 E. 50th Street
New York, NY 10022

LERNER PUBLICATIONS COMPANY
241 First Avenue North
Minneapolis, MN 55401

LITTLE, BROWN & COMPANY, INC.
34 Beacon Street
Boston, MA 02108

LOLLIPOP POWER BOOKS
P.O. Box 277
Carrboro, NC 27510

LOTHROP, LEE & SHEPARD BOOKS
105 Madison Avenue
New York, NY 10016

MACMILLAN PUBLISHING COMPANY
866 Third Avenue
New York, NY 10022

MARIPOSA PUBLISHING
922 Baca Street
Santa Fe, NM 87501

MODERN CURRICULUM PRESS
13900 Prospect Road
Cleveland, OH 44136

MORROW JUNIOR BOOKS
105 Madison Avenue
New York, NY 10016

WILLIAM MORROW AND COMPANY, INC.
1350 Avenue of the Americas
New York, NY 10019

NEW MEXICO MAGAZINE
1100 Saint Francis Drive
Sante Fe, NM 87503

PANTHEON BOOKS
201 East 50th Street
New York, NY 10022

RAINTREE PUBLISHERS
310 Wisconsin Avenue
Milwaukee, WI 53203

RANDOM HOUSE, INC.
201 E. 50th Street
New York, NY 10022

SCHOLASTIC, INC.
730 Broadway
New York, NY 10003

CHARLES SCRIBNER'S SONS
866 Third Avenue
New York, NY 10022

STATE HOUSE PRESS
P.O. Box 15247
Austin, TX 78761

STECK-VAUGHN COMPANY
P.O. Box 26015
Austin, TX 78755

TEXART, INC.
P.O. Box 15440
San Antonio, TX 78212

VIKING PENGUIN, INC.
40 W. 23rd Street
New York, NY 10016

WATERHILL PRESS
100 Corporate Drive
Mahwah, NJ 07430

ALBERT WHITMAN
5747 W. Howard Street
Niles, IL 60648

INDEX

AUTHOR / TITLE INDEX

SUBJECT INDEX